LAKE SUPERIOR

Agates
Field Guide
BY DAN R. LYNCH & BOB LYNCH

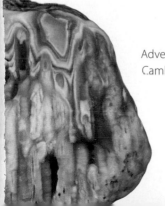

Adventure Publications
Cambridge, Minnesota

Dedication

To Nancy Lynch, wife of Bob and mother of Dan, for her love and continued support of our book projects.

And to Julie Kirsch, Dan's wife, for her love and patience.

Acknowledgments

Thanks to the following for providing specimens and/or information: Christopher Cordes, Terry Roses, Terry and Bobbi House, Eric Powers, Dave Woerheide and Alex Fagotti.

All photos by Dan R. Lynch, except page 9—Courtesy of Visible Earth, Jacques Descloitres, MODIS Rapid Response Team, NASA/GSFC (http://visibleearth.nasa.gov/)

Cover and book design by Jonathan Norberg

Edited by Brett Ortler

15 14 13 12 11 10

Lake Superior Agates Field Guide
Copyright © 2012 by Dan R. Lynch and Bob Lynch
Published by Adventure Publications
An imprint of AdventureKEEN
310 Garfield Street South
Cambridge, Minnesota 55008
(800) 678-7006
www.adventurepublications.net
All rights reserved
Printed in China
ISBN 978-1-59193-282-6 (pbk.)

Table of Contents

Introduction to Agates

What exactly is an agate? That's the primary question posed by most newcomers to the hobby of agate collecting. Agates are complex things; they form in vesicles (gas bubbles) in rocks and are a layered form of a very hard material called chalcedony (pronounced "kal-SED-oh-nee"), which is a particular variety of the mineral quartz. Like layers in an onion, an agate's layers are actually shells of chalcedony formed within each other. Breaking or cutting open an agate reveals the banding pattern for which agates are famous.

Identifying Agates

Agates are a variety of microcrystalline quartz (masses of quartz containing crystals too small to be seen), so while agates look nothing like quartz crystals, they still exhibit all the properties of quartz. So once you think you've found an agate, look carefully for the following characteristics, all of which are shared by quartz.

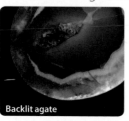
Backlit agate

TRANSLUCENCY
Though the trademark banding may seem like the primary identifying feature of an agate, other minerals can be banded. However, few banded minerals are also translucent like the

chalcedony in agates. Even large examples of agates will appear to "glow" when held in the sunlight; this phenomenon is often visible at a specimen's edges or in thin areas.

HARDNESS AND WAXY LUSTER

Quartz is an extremely hard mineral, and so agates are too. In fact, quartz and agates are the hardest materials you'll find in the Lake Superior region. They are so hard they can't be scratched by a steel knife. In addition, agates with freshly broken and weathered surfaces have a waxy luster or shine.

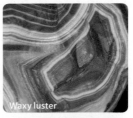

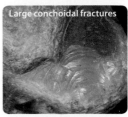
Waxy luster

CONCHOIDAL FRACTURE

Most minerals break in a particular way when struck. Quartz, along with many other hard, brittle minerals, has a conchoidal fracture, which means that semi-circular cracks and chips appear when struck or broken. Other forms of quartz exhibit this trait as well, so it isn't a foolproof identifier of an agate, but conchoidal fractures are so common on agate specimens that their presence certainly helps make identification easier. Thousands

Large conchoidal fractures

Small conchoidal fractures

of years of being exposed to glaciers and waves have created countless fractures on specimens for you to observe. Fresh fractures will appear light-colored, while old ones will be less obvious.

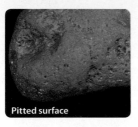

Pitted surface

PITTED OUTER SURFACES

When an agate is whole and shows no banding, identification can be difficult. Look for agate's usually waxy luster in addition to many pits and dimples on the outer surfaces of the specimen. These can occur in any size and were caused by minerals that protruded onto the agate as it formed within a vesicle.

Agate Look-alikes

Chalcedony and agates are not the only quartz varieties that can be found in the Lake Superior region, nor are they the most common. And because all of these quartz varieties can exhibit distinct layering, conchoidal fracture, waxy luster, and extreme hardness, there are many confusing agate look-alikes. But there are noticeable differences that can help you distinguish these imposters from actual agates.

CHERT

Chert is a type of sedimentary rock composed primarily of microscopic grains of quartz. It can contain agate-like layers, and is one of the materials most often confused with agates. Chert, however, is typically only found in shades of white, gray or brown and is opaque, not translucent like agates.

JASPER

Jasper is essentially a colored, iron-rich variety of chert. It too can contain agate-like layering. However, the layers in jasper are generally poorly defined and not circular. Unlike agate, jasper often appears grainy under magnification and is almost always opaque, not translucent.

JASPILITE

"Jaspilite" is the name collectors use to refer to jasper with parallel layers of hematite, an iron ore. When water-worn, specimens of jaspilite are frequently mistaken for agates, but agates never contain broad black metallic layers of hematite. Agates are also not quite so opaque.

Specimen courtesy of Dave Woerheide

STROMATOLITES

Stromatolites have waving, twisting layers that can resemble agate banding. Unlike in agates, stromatolite banding is rarely circular and is opaque. Stromatolites are fossilized remains of aquatic bacteria colonies that were preserved within chert and jasper.

RHYOLITE

Rhyolite is an opaque volcanic rock that occasionally exhibits parallel stripes of color. Though sometimes confused with agate, these streaks are not quartz and were caused by the direction of the flowing lava.

Specimen courtesy of Alex Fagotti

Where to Find Agates

Long after Lake Superior agates formed, glaciers moved them far and wide. Today, agates can be found all over the region. The map to the left shows the primary range of Lake Superior agates.

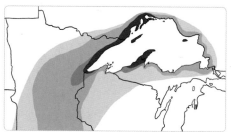
Lake Superior agate range

The darkest red coloration indicates areas where agates actually formed. The varying shades of pink show concentrations of agates moved by the glaciers and rivers. When hunting for agates in these areas, your best chances will be where earth/soil is being moved, making the following locations great places to start:

- Lake Superior's shoreline is always a popular place to look, but agates found there are typically small and heavily weathered, though they are easy to spot and identify.

- Riverbanks and beds, whether part of a large river or small stream, are always good places to look because dirt is always moving and uncovering new material.

- Gravel pits in the region consist purely of glacial till (rocks left behind by glaciers) and can contain countless agates, some quite large. Nearly all gravel pits are privately owned, and gravel pits can be quite dangerous, so ask for permission and be wary of large, loose rock piles or cliffs.

Protected and Private Land

Our region has dozens of state parks and forests, Native American reservations and nationally protected parks and monuments, all of which are areas where it is illegal to collect anything. Large fines await those caught collecting in protected areas. We encourage collectors to obey the law and leave these natural spaces wild and untouched for generations to come. It is your responsibility to know whether or not the area in which you are collecting is protected. In addition, many potential collecting sites are privately owned, including many parts of the Lake Superior shoreline. Needless to say, if you collect on private property you are trespassing, and the penalty may be worse than just a fine. In addition, property lines change frequently, as do owners, so just because a landowner gave you permission to collect on their property last year it doesn't mean that the new owner will allow you on their property the next year.

The Geological History of the Region

To better understand how Lake Superior agates formed, it helps to know the basic geology of the region and the events that produced Lake Superior as we know it. Lake Superior is the largest freshwater lake in the world in terms of surface area, but it is only about 10,000 years old. Believe it or not, that's young, geologically speaking. The rock beneath the lake is much older, and formed approximately 1.1 billion years ago. At the time, North

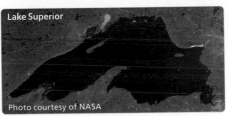

Lake Superior

Photo courtesy of NASA

9

America was part of a large landmass called Rodinia, which was beginning to split apart. This created a large gap, called a rift. If this rift had been successful, a sea would have formed. Instead, molten rock filled in the gap and hardened into massive sheets of rock. (Geologically, this event is referred to as the "Midcontinent Rift.") As the huge rock formations cooled, they contracted, forming what would much later become the Lake Superior basin. Soon after the rocks cooled, Lake Superior agates began forming within vesicles (gas bubbles) in them.

Ice Ages and Glaciers

Over time, the rocks of the Midcontinent Rift (and the agates in them) were buried. They were not uncovered until about 110,000 years ago, when the world plunged into an ice age. Ice ages are characterized by low global temperatures and the advance of massive glaciers. As the enormous, mile-thick sheets of ice descended from Canada, they scoured the Lake Superior region, unburying the rocks bearing the region's agates. But they didn't just uncover the rock, they crushed countless tons of it, but the extremely hard agates within them survived. The ice sheets then transported agates all over the region, burying

Glacial activity

them in glacially deposited gravel (called glacial till). This diagram illustrates the glacial activity in the region during the last ice age. The dark blue shading indicates the extent of the very last glaciers and the arrows show their direction of movement. The light blue shading illustrates the extent of earlier glaciers.

At the end of the ice age about 10,000 years ago, the glaciers retreated and the remnants they left behind melted, filling the Lake Superior basin with water.

Agate Formation

Agate formation is one of the most compelling remaining mysteries in the geological sciences. Since agates form within cavities in solid rock, their formation has never been directly observed. Even so, we have some promising theories.

Because agates are chalcedony, a special variety of quartz, it's easier to understand agate formation if you know a little bit about quartz. Quartz is a mineral, not a rock. Simply put, minerals are the solidified form of a pure chemical compound. Quartz is a mixture of the elements silicon and oxygen and is actually the most abundant mineral on earth. Because it is so common, quartz is often referred to simply as silica, a catch-all term for any quartz-based material. For the purposes of this book, silica often refers to the liquid solution from which quartz forms.

Minnesota quartz crystal

Because quartz is present in virtually every geological environment, it can take a number of different crystal shapes. Chalcedony is one such variety of quartz; it consists of countless

11

plate-like crystals too small to see with the naked eye. Chalcedony formation is not fully understood, but it seems to develop only in environments with a low temperature, low pressure and high acidity. Researchers think that Lake Superior's chalcedony formed when volcanic activity generated mineral-rich water and steam, which made contact with the recently cooled volcanic rocks.

Basalt

Agate still embedded in rock

Lake Superior agates primarily developed in two types of volcanic rocks: basalt and rhyolite. Most formed in basalt, a dense, extremely fine-grained rock very common along Lake Superior. Often black, gray or dark green, basalt can range in size from pebbles to entire cliffs.

Both rhyolite and basalt had cooled very quickly, and this trapped gases within them. These gas bubbles formed hollow cavities (called vesicles) where minerals could form. When mineral-rich water and steam contacted the rock, it began to react. This created a thin coating of two soft, green clay-like minerals (chlorite and celadonite) on the inside of the cavities.

Dissolved silica in the water then collected on these soft minerals. This silica began to clump (nucleate) around small points on the inside of the cavity. Tiny chalcedony spheres (called spherulites) grew from these points until they formed the outermost chalcedony layer of an agate, called the husk, which is different from every other layer.

Thick outer chalcedony layer, or "husk"

Celadonite-coated agate in basalt

Specimen courtesy of Jim Cordes

From there, the agate formed inward. While theorists generally understand the early phases of agate formation, it's not clear at all how interior banding develops.

Part of the problem is most agates have three distinct types of bands: (1) impurity-stained chalcedony bands, which are often red or brown (2) thin, white and opaque bands of purer chalcedony and (3) clear, colorless bands of microscopic quartz grains. These bands typically repeat in a perfect alternating pattern, indicating that a highly organized process created the layers in an agates. But the cause of this process is widely debated.

While the details are quite complicated, an emerging theory states that an acidic silica solution began to cling together, forming a layer of silica-rich gel on the inside of the husk. Through an elaborate process, the layer of gel hardened into the three bands discussed above. When more silica entered the cavity, the process continued until the vesicle was full of chalcedony bands, forming an agate. Studies have shown that chalcedony takes a great amount of silica to form, so if there wasn't enough silica during formation, macrocrystalline quartz formed instead. Macrocrystalline quartz is a quartz formation with crystals large enough to see with the naked eye, and it is common at the center of agates.

Macrocrystalline quartz center

Lake Superior Agate Varieties

Any novice who has attended an agate sale has heard veteran collectors utter phrases like "water-washed sagenite" and "paint floater" in reference to Lake Superior agates. These are examples of the many varieties of agates found in the region, and although the labels may seem cryptic and identification intimidating at first, learning about and acquiring the many varieties is what makes Lake Superior agate collecting so interesting and rewarding. And there are many varieties to be had. Many other factors can affect an agate's formation and its eventual appearance, leading collectors to classify it as a specific agate variety. Such variables include the presence of other crystals in the cavity, color-causing impurities in an agate, differences in the silica solution during formation, and even how ice, wind and waves eroded a specimen. Dozens of these varieties exist and all of the most significant are detailed in this book.

STRUCTURAL VARIATIONS

There are many varieties established by collectors, most determined by appearance alone, but agate researchers and scientists consider there to be only a few true varieties of agates. These varieties are structurally different from one another, and their differences stem from the physical arrangement and organization of their banding patterns. For example, fortification agates, also often called adhesional banded agates, are the common agates that exhibit the classic concentric, band-within-a-band pattern, while water-level agates contain flat, parallel horizontal layering. Obviously, these examples have very distinct structural differences. Such structural differences were determined early on by the state of the silica entering the vesicle, the conditions in the surrounding rock, and other unknown factors.

INCLUSIONS

Agates require a large amount of material and very specific conditions in order to form, but other minerals that grow in vesicles are much less finicky. Zeolites and calcite, for example, are minerals that form more easily and more quickly than agates, which means that crystals of such minerals grew both before and during agate formation. The result is agates that contain unusual structures that cause the agate banding to bend and warp around them. Agates also sometimes contain unusual materials, such as copper, embedded within them. And while not every agate contains inclusions, countless agates do.

COLOR VARIATIONS

When it comes to the colors seen in Lake Superior agates, there are few surprises. The vast majority contain the usual iron-stained shades of brown, red and yellow, along with white and gray. But other rarer colorations and color combinations exist and are noteworthy enough that collectors consider them to be a different agate variety. And rarer still, certain sought-after color variations can occur together in a single specimen.

WEATHERING EFFECTS

Nearly every Lake Superior agate shows signs of weathering (unless very recently removed from its host rock). The most prominent evidence of weathering is the slight rounding, smoothing and cracking caused by the immense weight of the glaciers. But some forms of weathering are much more unique, and these weathering effects include everything from completely smoothed water-washed agates to those that have been crushed and cemented together.

Labeling Your Finds

When attempting to determine what type of agate you have, begin by looking at the banding and its characteristics. This will help you determine an agate's structural variety, of which it will only have one. Then take note of any inclusions it may have as well as any unusual colors and weathering. For example, a specimen may contain many types of inclusions but show no unique weathering.

Your agate will exhibit only one of the following structural variations:

 Common band-within-a-band concentric pattern, sometimes with a center of coarse quartz crystals — **Fortification Agate**, page 23

 A thin shell of agate bands surrounding a large mass of quartz with distinct layers — **Banded Quartz Agate**, page 41

 Perfectly circular banded spots on the outer surfaces of a specimen — **Eye Agate**, page 83

 Regions of banded chalcedony completely surrounded by thick layers of macrocrystalline quartz — **Floater Agate**, page 49

 Specimens with a hollow center, often lined with countless tiny crystals — **Agate Geode**, page 95

 Parallel bands at the bottom of a specimen, often with quartz above — **Water-level Agate**, page 35

Opaque white to grayish blue quartz with a distinctly "crackly" appearance

Skip-an-Atom Agate, page 133

Long, narrow banded patterns lacking the usual rounded shape

Vein Agate, page 111

Lumpy, wavy bands in semi-circular arrangements and composed primarily of white chalcedony

Whorl Agate, page 145

Your agate may contain one or more of the following types of inclusions (or none at all):

Small agate nodules coated in green chlorite and containing pale chalcedony and solid copper bands

Copper Replacement Agate, page 121

Smooth-walled geometrically shaped holes in the outer surfaces of an agate

Crystal Impressions, page 45

Microscopically thin red or yellow tree-like shapes in between the bands of an agate

Dendritic Agate, page 79

Soft, opaque, curling ribbon-like fragments of material typically separated from the agate banding

Fragmented Membrane Agate, page 91

Irregular masses of opaque jasper alongside typical banded agate

Jasp-Agate, page 53

Geometric masses embedded in an agate that are typically softer and differently colored

Mineral Inclusions, page 57

Tangles of thin, filament-like tubes that resemble moss embedded within chalcedony

Moss Agate, page 27

 Small, branching, tree-like growths that extend deeper into non-banded chalcedony

Plume Agate, page 125

 Circular arrangements of needle-like crystal inclusions

Sagenitic Agate, page 103

 Slender, icicle-like tube shapes extending only partway through an agate

Stalactitic Agate, page 107

 Slender tubes, sometimes hollow, that extend from one side of an agate through to the other

Tube Agate, page 65

Your agate may exhibit some of the following color variations (or none at all):

 Masses of coarse quartz crystals in shades of purple, gray, yellow, brown or green

Colored Macrocrystalline Quartz, page 75

 Agates with opaque coloration, particularly in shades of orange, tan, brown and pink

Paint Agate, page 61

 Agate banding of strange coloration, such as dark green, purple and pink, often in combination

Rare Colorations, page 129

 Yellow, red or white coloration in a thin coating on an agate's outer surfaces

Surface Colorations, page 31

Broken fragments of a banded agate that have been cemented together by another material

Brecciated Agate, page 71

 Agates containing large cracks that disrupt banding, causing shifted, mismatched bands

Faulted Agate, page 87

 Flat, smooth, evenly colored and non-banded surface texture

Peeled Agate, page 99

 Unusually smooth, worn surfaces that appear shiny, as if polished

Ventifacts, page 141

 Very smooth, rounded, pebble-shaped agates showing banding on all sides

Water-washed Agate, page 115

Remember that an agate will only have one structural variation, despite the fact that a specimen may appear to show traits of several. For example, a specimen may show all the signs of being a floater agate, but if it has a hollow center, then it is still considered to be an agate geode. In contrast, an agate may have many types of inclusions present, while another specimen may have none at all. Similarly, unique color variations and signs of weathering may or may not be present. When you have determined what variations are present in a specimen, it can then be given a detailed label. For example, an agate with ample layered quartz and tube structures would typically be labeled a "banded quartz tube agate." Finally, only the most unique signs of weathering and colorations are included on this chart, and many agates will not exhibit these specific traits, instead exhibiting only the more common agate appearance.

Very Common

The most abundant and most easily found types of Lake Superior agates

There are a few kinds of Lake Superior agates that take little effort to find. Whether they're found on beaches, in rivers or in the rock piles of gravel pits, fortification agates, water-level agates, moss agates and agates with various surface colorations are abundant and turn up virtually anywhere agates are found.

Fortification Agate
(pg. 23)

Moss Agate
(pg. 27)

Surface Colorations
(pg. 31)

Water-level Agate
(pg. 35)

Fortification Agate

Primary Range

SYNONYMS: Common agate, classic agate, fort agate, wall-lining agate, zonally concentric banding agate, adhesional banded agate

CHARACTERISTIC FEATURES:
- Solid bands that completely encircle each other and follow the contours of the agate's general shape
- Shape of individual bands gradually becomes smoother as they progress inward
- Bands can be of any color, but typically alternate between colored bands and white or colorless bands

RARITY: Fortification agates are the most common variety, and most agates you'll find throughout the Lake Superior region will be of this type

DESCRIPTION: The most common agate worldwide, fortification agates are what everyone thinks of when the word "agate" is mentioned. Technically known as adhesional banded agates, these agates get their common name because their bands resemble the walls of a fort or castle as viewed from above. The more technical scientific name is often used to avoid the confusion that results from this widespread agate's many common names.

Unpolished agate with highly desirable red and white coloration

Concentric bands

23

Fortification agates exhibit the classic concentric, band-within-a-band pattern for which agates are famous. These agates feature all of the aspects one expects to see in an agate. In fact, they are the variety that is studied almost exclusively by researchers. This is because fortification agates formed from the most ideal set of agate-producing conditions and were uninterrupted during growth, producing their perfect banding pattern. These most popular of Lake Superior agates can also be found in any color, shape and size, making extraordinary specimens particularly exciting to collectors.

IDENTIFICATION: Identification of fortification agates is simple due to their sheer abundance. With the exception of water-level agates (page 35) and their parallel layers, virtually every banded agate you'll find will be a fortification agate or a closely related variety. If a specimen you've found is broken in a way that the banding pattern is easily visible, simply look for the classic concentric bands completely encircling each other. A body of macrocrystalline quartz often lies at the center of these agates. Occasionally the bands appear "lopsided" and are thinner on one side of the pattern than the other, but the same features are still evident in all examples.

COLLECTIBILITY: Even though they are the most common type of Lake Superior agate, no other variety is as valuable or as sought after by collectors. In fact, some truly extraordinary specimens can be worth thousands of dollars. But their abundance means that the line between "priceless" and "worthless" is a thin one. Serious collectors

Macrocrystalline quartz center

scrutinize every aspect of a specimen to ensure that it meets all the criteria that make an agate exceptional. These characteristics aren't always apparent, leading novices to often wonder why one agate is worth more than another. When it comes to any Lake Superior agate, and especially fortification agates, the size or weight of the specimen are not the most important factors, though they are always considered. Other characteristics have more impact on value, such as contrast between bands, completeness of pattern, the amount or type of inclusions, the macrocrystalline quartz content, and the overall aesthetics of a specimen. For example, agates with bright, high-contrast red and white bands and very little quartz are highly desired.

Dark gray agate

COMPARE & CONTRAST:

Agate Geode	Floater Agate	Water-level Agate	Vein Agate
Similar banding but with a hollow center	Similar banding but with large quartz layers	Parallel horizontal bands	Elongated patterns with rough exteriors

WHERE TO BEGIN LOOKING: Some of the finest examples have come from gravel pits and farm fields all over Minnesota, especially near Duluth, Two Harbors, Cloquet and even the Twin Cities, while the shores of inland lakes everywhere are also lucrative. Specimens are also common on virtually all of Lake Superior's shores.

Polished moss agate

Moss-like growths

Macrocrystalline quart

Moss Agate

SYNONYMS: Tree agate

Primary Range

CHARACTERISTIC FEATURES:

- Masses of chalcedony containing tangled filament-like growths that can greatly resemble organic moss

- Under magnification, the moss-like growths typically resemble hollow tubes

- Regions of banded chalcedony can exist, but generally only as isolated pockets surrounded by moss-like growths

- Moss agates can occasionally be very large

RARITY: Moss agates both large and small are very common in the Lake Superior region, much to the chagrin of collectors

DESCRIPTION: Moss agates were one of the first agate varieties discovered, and the first references to them date back to the ancient Greeks, over 2,000 years ago. Among the most common agate varieties in the Lake Superior region, moss agates are technically not agates. Generally speaking, for a specimen to be called a "true" agate, it must have the classic concentric or horizontal chalcedony banding. Moss agates, however, rarely exhibit banding. Instead they contain wild, moss-like patterns of mineral growths that look strangely organic, all within a mass of chalcedony. In fact, until 1776,

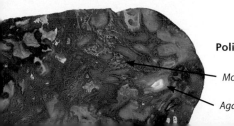

Polished moss agate

Moss-like growths

Agate banding

27

researchers were convinced that moss agates actually contained fossilized moss. Today we know that the "moss" in moss agates is actually the result of a complex chemical reaction between iron compounds and a body of silica (quartz). But they are obviously very different from standard agates, so why are they considered agates at all? Mostly, it's due to tradition—moss agates have always been considered agates—but they also formed in a manner similar to normal agates. Occasionally pockets of normal agate banding are present between the mossy growths in a specimen. This indicates that moss agates formed under similar conditions and in close to the same manner.

IDENTIFICATION: Moss agates are one of the most abundant varieties of Lake Superior agates, so you've likely already come across one. When cut or polished, moss agates are immediately identifiable, but when in their natural, highly weathered state, it can be much more difficult to recognize them. Many inexperienced collectors find what they think is a large agate-like mass of chalcedony only to later have it identified as a nearly worthless moss agate. To avoid this disappointment, try wetting a specimen in water or mineral oil to help reveal the details hidden below the surface damage a specimen may exhibit. If you see mottled coloration, mossy structures and a lack of banding, you have a moss agate. If still in doubt, use magnification—the twisting moss structures in agates are actually tiny tubes.

Unpolished moss agate

COLLECTIBILITY: The cultural significance of moss agates dates back to ancient Greece, so it may seem ironic that they are one of the most valueless and least beloved varieties of Lake Superior agate. But within the sphere of serious Lake Superior agate collectors, well-formed, high-contrast adhesional bands are the most desired, so the "messy" appearance of moss agates is off-putting for most discerning hobbyists. Monetary concerns aside, however, polished moss agates can be truly beautiful in their complexity and they do have many advocates, particularly among collectors who specialize in "weird" agates. In general, however, moss agates (even those that are very large) are relatively worthless when compared to banded agates.

Close-up of "moss"

COMPARE & CONTRAST:

Fragmented Membrane Agate	Tube Agate	Jasp-Agate
Inclusions are separate curved ribbons	Inclusions are less plentiful and are clearly tube-like	Banding within opaque jasper

WHERE TO BEGIN LOOKING: You'll find moss agates everywhere around Lake Superior, but the shoreline between Two Harbors and Grand Marais, Minnesota, is often very lucrative. Moss agates are very widespread and can even be found along rivers in the Twin Cities.

Polished agate with surface coloration

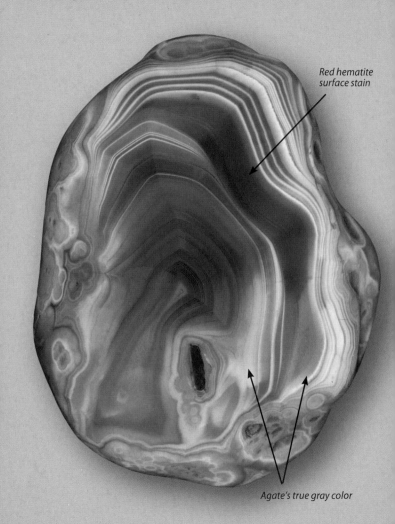

Red hematite surface stain

Agate's true gray color

Surface Colorations

Primary Range

SYNONYMS: Surface staining

CHARACTERISTIC FEATURES:

- Thin coatings of red, yellow or white on the outermost surfaces of an agate
- In highly weathered areas, the surface coloration may be worn away to reveal an agate's true coloration below
- Red and yellow surface staining typically doesn't affect white chalcedony bands

RARITY: Red and yellow surface colorations are very common, while white surface coloration is fairly uncommon

DESCRIPTION: Lake Superior agates can be full of surprises. An inexperienced collector might eagerly polish their newest discovery only to watch in dismay as the beautiful reds and yellows change to gray as the surface of the agate is ground down. This is not an uncommon occurrence, but why? The answer has to do with an agate's structure. Chalcedony is porous, and tiny, microscopic spaces exist within its structure. Impurities are trapped within these spaces and contribute to an agate's coloration. When an agate free from its host rock remains buried, particularly within glacial till, it comes into contact with iron-bearing groundwater. Over time,

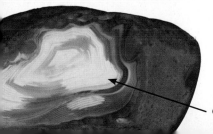

Polished agate with white surface bleaching

Chemically bleached bands

the outer surfaces of an agate that has contacted enough water will take on the reddish hues of hematite or the mustard-yellow coloration of limonite, and rarely both. But this coloration is only skin-deep, which is why polishing or even chipping the surface of a specimen will quickly reveal the true coloration. Interestingly, the white chalcedony bands in an agate often retain their color even when the other nearby banding is heavily discolored. This occurs because those bands are the densest and most resilient to staining. In some agates, acidic water has removed color-causing impurities, producing a white surface coloration in a process called bleaching.

IDENTIFICATION: Initially, identifying agates with "false" colorations may seem difficult, but there are a few key traits to watch out for. Though damage is never appreciated in any agate specimen, breaks and fractures can actually help to identify an agate with surface colorations. Because the coloration is so thin, even a small chip is often deep enough to reveal the true coloration below. And since the staining or bleaching of these agates undoubtedly took place thousands of years ago, you certainly won't have to purposely damage a specimen yourself because there should be ample cracks and chips already present, thanks to weathering. Identification is then a simple matter of determining if the interior color matches the outer surface color or not.

Limonite surface coating (yellow)

Unpolished agate with surface colorations

Hematite surface coating (red)

COLLECTIBILITY: Lake Superior agates with surface colorations are not particularly sought after. Any collector, novice or professional, would much rather have an agate that exhibited its true coloration, rather than a thin surface coating, because it significantly limits what you can do with the agate. For example, an agate may have a beautiful red color, but a collector can never polish it or that coloration will wear away. Still, some of these agates can be collectible. There are countless examples in which red and yellow staining or white bleaching have enhanced an agate's otherwise drab and uninteresting gray or brown coloration. Finally, expert polishing techniques can carefully remove a small amount of the surface coloration, allowing the true coloration to show through while retaining some of the staining, making for very desirable specimens.

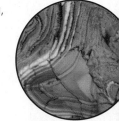

Limonite surface coating

Limonite surface coating

COMPARE & CONTRAST:

Paint Agate	Rare Colorations

Coloration is not just on outer surfaces | Coloration is not just on outer surfaces

WHERE TO BEGIN LOOKING: Gravel pits around Cloquet and Duluth, Minnesota, often produce agates with surface colorations, as do lakeshores in northeastern Minnesota.

Polished water-level agate

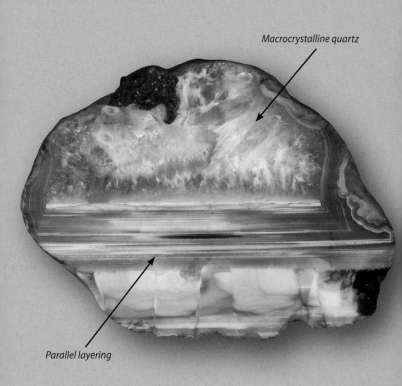

Macrocrystalline quartz

Parallel layering

Water-level Agate

Primary Range

SYNONYMS: Onyx, horizontally banded agate, Uruguay-type agate

CHARACTERISTIC FEATURES:
- Parallel, horizontal layers at the bottom of an agate
- Horizontal layers often turn into concentric bands at the outer edges of an agate
- A mass of coarse crystalline quartz often fills the area above the horizontal layers
- Occasionally, the horizontal layers change color and texture along their length, exhibiting a mosaic-like quality

RARITY: Water-level agates are not uncommon, but are less abundant than fortification agates

DESCRIPTION: Geologists consider there to be only two true types of agates: those with concentric banding and agates with gravitational banding. Most banded agates are variations of the fortification agate, but water-level agates are a unique type of agate. Technically known as gravitationally banded agates, Lake Superior agate collectors know them better as water-level agates and historians know them as onyx. These agates clearly formed from a process dependent on gravity, as nothing else could have produced the perfectly flat, parallel layers they exhibit. It is thought that

Unpolished water-level agate

the silica solution that contributed to the formation of water-level agates contained too much water and was too "runny" to adhere to the walls of the vesicle. The silica then clumped together in heavy particles that sank to the bottom of the vesicle (cavity), settling into parallel layers. What is unclear, however, is why some of the horizontal layers change color and texture along their length or exactly why many of the horizontal layers turn into common concentric bands at a specimen's edges.

IDENTIFICATION: The water-level agates' parallel horizontal layers are dramatically different than those of the common fortification agate (page 23). Since most kinds of Lake Superior agates are variations of the fortification agate and have concentric bands that encircle each other, it's easy to see how water-level agates are different. Their appearance is so distinct that even novices should have no trouble instantly identifying one of these agates. Most of the time, the horizontal layers in water-level agates do not fill an entire specimen, only part of it. More often than not, a large mass of macrocrystalline quartz resides above the parallel layers. Occasionally these agates exhibit common concentric banding, or more rarely, a geode cavity, but no matter what is found above the horizontal banding, all agates with flat, parallel bands are considered water-level agates. This is true whether there is only one small horizontal band in a specimen or many large ones.

Unpolished water-level agate

COLLECTIBILITY: Water-level agates are highly collectible and help diversify an agate collection. But these agates are not rare, so as with any agate type, the most desirable specimens are those with well-defined and colorful, high-contrast bands. Other unique features, such as agate eyes or mineral inclusions, can help a specimen's appeal as well. Perhaps one of the most intriguing traits of these agates is that we always know how the agate was oriented during formation; thanks to gravity and the horizontal bands, we always know which way is up. Though typically not as valuable as fortification agates, water-level agates are scientifically significant and no collection is complete without one.

Polished agate

COMPARE & CONTRAST:

Tube Agate	Vein Agate	Fortification Agate
Parallel structures are sparse and unevenly spaced	Flat, narrow bands are often present, but aren't perfectly parallel	Concentric banding

WHERE TO BEGIN LOOKING: Water-level agates are abundant throughout the entire Lake Superior region. Small but beautifully weathered specimens are very common all along Lake Superior's shore in Minnesota and Wisconsin.

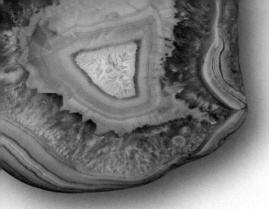

Common

While these agates are not the most abundant types, they're still fairly easy to find and identify

There are several common types of Lake Superior agates with unique colors and embedded crystals. Many of these varieties are the result of inclusions of other minerals. The other common agate variations listed here result from chemical changes during formation, but all are fairly abundant and widespread throughout the region.

Banded Quartz Agate (pg. 41)

Crystal Impressions (pg. 45)

Floater Agate (pg. 49)

Jasp-Agate (pg. 53)

Mineral Inclusions (pg. 57)

Paint Agate (pg. 61)

Tube Agate (pg. 65)

Polished banded quartz agate

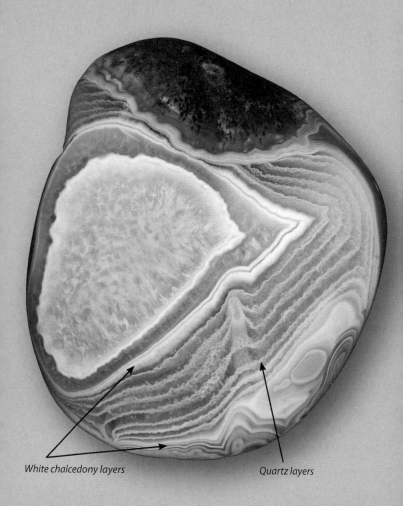

White chalcedony layers

Quartz layers

Banded Quartz Agate

Primary Range

SYNONYMS: Quartz ball, quartzy agate

CHARACTERISTIC FEATURES:

- Large amounts of coarse quartz grains or crystals arranged into layers
- Few chalcedony bands, typically only on the outer edges of the specimen and rarely deeper inside
- The distinction between quartz layers is often faint and poorly defined

RARITY: Banded quartz agates are a common type of Lake Superior agates and are found throughout the region

DESCRIPTION: Serious collectors favor agates that contain only banded chalcedony and have very little macrocrystalline quartz. This is why these "quartz balls," as collectors call them, are often viewed as undesirable. But banded quartz agates can be interesting and attractive in their own right. They typically consist of a large center of layered macrocrystalline or granular quartz surrounded by a thin outer coating of chalcedony banding. In these agates, the interior mass of quartz generally has faint yet distinct banding, which signifies distinct periods of crystal growth. Rarely, thin layers of chalcedony form between some of the quartz layers. The distinct

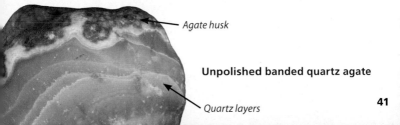

Agate husk

Unpolished banded quartz agate

Quartz layers

41

layering present in these agates reflects changes in the silica levels as the agates developed. This makes banded quartz agates a great illustration of the varying conditions that existed during agate formation. While not all collectors see the virtues of banded quartz agates, many enjoy them because specimens are often large but remain translucent, and the quartz often appears to "glow" from within when placed in the sun. The "spiky" boundaries of the quartz bands are another interesting feature of these stones; the peaks are actually crystal points.

IDENTIFICATION: Banded quartz agates are a variety of fortification agate (page 23), and many fortification Lake Superior agates contain large cores of macrocrystalline quartz. Not all quartz centers are banded, but determining whether you've found a banded quartz agate is easy, just look to see if the quartz shows signs of layering. The quartz bands can be very faint and poorly defined, but there is often a thin ribbon of lighter-colored quartz at the boundary of the banding, making it easier to see. Nevertheless, one can only look for banding if an agate has been broken or weathered enough to reveal the interior banding. Since most banded quartz agates have a thin outer shell of banded chalcedony, it can be impossible to identify one's find if the agate is whole and unbroken. This is likely the reason that some collectors have come to despise these "quartz balls." Banded quartz agates are often the largest of all Lake Superior agates, so it can be disappointing to cut open a large nodule to find a virtually worthless mass of quartz.

Polished banded quartz agate

COLLECTIBILITY: Unless they are exceptionally well formed or have particularly interesting features or inclusions, banded quartz agates typically hold little value and catch few collectors' eyes. Even very large specimens typically are not desirable or valuable. Each collector's personal tastes vary, of course, but most serious Lake Superior agate hobbyists seek out more "solid" agates that contain little or no macrocrystalline quartz and as much chalcedony banding as possible. Some collectors do, however, appreciate the translucency displayed by the quartz, which can give polished agates an incredible sense of depth.

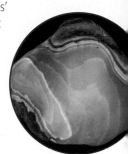

Lighter-colored boundaries between quartz layers

COMPARE & CONTRAST:

Floater Agate	Colored Macrocrystalline Quartz	Fortification Agate	Skip-an-Atom Agate
Ample quartz, but far more chalcedony banding	Bodies of quartz are colored	Ample chalcedony banding with little quartz	Quartz is opaque and grayish blue

WHERE TO BEGIN LOOKING: These common agates can be found anywhere in the region, but particularly in gravel pits and riverbeds near Duluth, Minnesota, and Superior, Wisconsin. Lake Superior's shores in Ontario and the eastern portion of Michigan's Upper Peninsula yield specimens as well.

Polished agate with crystal impression

Calcite impression

Crystal Impressions

SYNONYMS: Crystal imprints

Primary Range

CHARACTERISTIC FEATURES:
- Distinct cavities or indentations in the surface of an agate, often taking the form of geometric shapes
- Chalcedony banding often warps and bends around the cavities
- Blocky or hexagonal (six-sided) cavities are most common

RARITY: Certain mineral impression shapes are more abundant than others, but all are common in Lake Superior's agates

DESCRIPTION: Even if you're a novice, it won't take long before you come across an agate with a distinctly shaped cavity in its outer husk or within its interior pattern. These cavities are clearly different than those seen in other agates (such as the agate geode, page 95). Such peculiar geometric holes are called crystal impressions, but don't let the name fool you; the crystals did not actually press into the agate. Actually, the opposite is true: crystals of other minerals formed simultaneously with the agate, and the agate banding bent and warped around the crystals. In the Lake Superior region, these crystals primarily consisted of calcite, barite, and various members of the zeolite group, all of which are somewhat soft and were later

Unpolished agate with large calcite crystal impression and cast made from that cavity

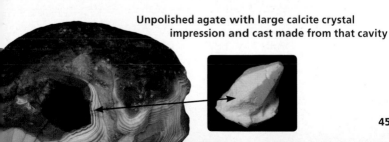

45

washed away by acidic water. The agate, however, was unaffected by the acid and remained intact. This resulted in agates with crystal-shaped voids that often appear to "push" the banding out of the way, forcing it to wrap around them. Not all crystal impressions are well formed and easily distinguishable. Some are the result of a mass of crystals and therefore exhibit numerous intergrown shapes, sometimes appearing as a crude "mess" of impressions.

IDENTIFICATION: Lake Superior agates are often pitted and dimpled. Some of these deformities were created when the agate formed, while others resulted from weathering, but only crystal impressions exhibit distinct geometric shapes. Impressions are often square, rectangular or hexagonal, but can be any other distinct shape. When trying to determine if the cavity in a specimen is a crystal impression, first compare it to the cavity at the center of an agate geode (page 95). Agate geodes do not exhibit a distinct angular shape and the cavities are always at the center of an agate. In addition, geode cavities are often lined with many tiny quartz crystals whereas the interiors of crystal impressions are virtually always smooth and free of additional mineral growths, except in rare cases. Determining which mineral made the impression is more difficult. First, use a field guide to compare the shape of the cavity with that of mineral crystals from the region. If it's difficult to picture the original mineral's shape, try making a cast of the cavity from clay or silicone.

Unpolished agate with calcite impression

COLLECTIBILITY: Like many Lake Superior agate oddities, crystal impressions garner only limited attention from collectors. Typically, only hobbyists who seek strange, unique agates will be attracted to agates with deep and obvious impressions. Collectors of traditional agate types generally dislike large crystal impressions, which often distract from the banded portions of a specimen. If the impressions on an agate are small, on the backside of the specimen, or don't distract from the banding, they are often ignored. It is only when a crystal impression is remarkably well formed and adds to the visual interest and overall aesthetics of a specimen that it becomes valuable.

Barite crystal impression

COMPARE & CONTRAST:

Agate Geodes	Tube Agate	Mineral Inclusions
Hollow cavity is not geometric in shape and is at the center of the banding	Round channels that extend deep into an agate	Geometric shapes that are not hollow

WHERE TO BEGIN LOOKING: Impressions are best found in agates that are weathered, but not worn smooth, making gravel pits near Duluth and Cloquet, Minnesota, lucrative sites.

Exceptional unpolished floater agate

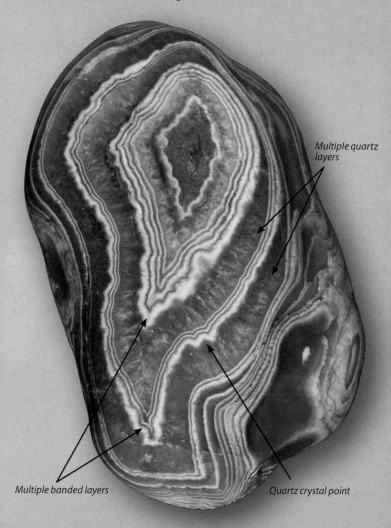

Multiple quartz layers

Multiple banded layers

Quartz crystal point

Floater Agate

SYNONYMS: Floater, suspended-center agate, suspended-banding agate

Primary Range

CHARACTERISTIC FEATURES:
- Regions of chalcedony banding surrounded by thick bands of coarse quartz crystals
- A single region of chalcedony banding surrounded by quartz may exist at the center of a specimen, or banded chalcedony sections may alternate with layers of coarse quartz crystals

RARITY: Floater agates are fairly common in the entire Lake Superior region, but are not quite as abundant as fortification agates

DESCRIPTION: While the name "floater agate" was invented by collectors and is not a scientific term, there is no better way to describe the "islands" of banded chalcedony that seem to float in masses of quartz in these agates. While they all contain ample amounts of chalcedony and quartz, there are two types of floater agates. Some consist of a single central mass of chalcedony surrounded by one body of quartz, while others consist of alternating regions of banded chalcedony and quartz, creating several "floating" bands. As chalcedony requires much more silica to form than macrocrystalline quartz, the varying amounts of each in a floater agate reflect dramatic rises and falls in the amount of available silica during the agate's

Unpolished floater agate

formation. These wild swings in silica content led to the formation of large individual quartz crystals within the macrocrystalline quartz, creating jagged boundaries between the chalcedony and quartz layers. When the chalcedony resumed forming, it filled in around these crystal points, preserving their shapes. These unique jagged borders are found in almost all specimens.

IDENTIFICATION: Floater agates are a variation of fortification agates (page 23), and as such they contain the common band-within-a-band agate structure. But unlike classic fortification agates, some of the bands within floaters are composed entirely of coarse macrocrystalline quartz. This is the first thing to look for when identifying these agates. The macrocrystalline quartz is always evident in both floater agate types, and the quartz layers are typically quite thick and noticeably more plentiful in floater agates than in fortification agates. The banded quartz agate (page 41) is the only agate type you're likely to easily mistake for a floater agate, but that's only likely if a specimen is nearly whole and doesn't show much of its interior pattern. Banded quartz agates contain little to no interior chalcedony banding and instead exhibit a large central mass of macrocrystalline quartz, so if only a small, shallow portion of an agate's interior is visible and only macrocrystalline quartz can be seen, it could be a banded quartz agate, or it could be a floater agate with the chalcedony bands hidden deeper within. If there are few other clues, only cutting the agate will reveal its identity.

Banded agate layers

Polished floater agate

Quartz layer

COLLECTIBILITY: Normally just called "floaters" by collectors, floater agates are often visually interesting and can be very collectible when colorful. But as with any variety of Lake Superior agate, many collectors dislike floaters that contain excessive amounts of macrocrystalline quartz. However, with the right balance of chalcedony banding, macrocrystalline quartz thickness, and vivid coloration, floaters can be very desirable and valuable.

Unpolished agate

COMPARE & CONTRAST:

Banded Quartz Agate	Agate Geode	Fortification Agate	Skip-an-Atom Agate
More quartz and less chalcedony banding	Can exhibit quartz bands, but has a hollow center	No large quartz bands	Quartz bands are opaque and grayish blue

WHERE TO BEGIN LOOKING: As one of the most common types of agate, floaters can be found anywhere in the region. Gravel pits near Cloquet, Minnesota, are very lucrative, as is Ontario's Lake Superior shoreline.

Unpolished jasp-agate

Jasper masses

Agate banding

Jasp-Agate

SYNONYMS: Jasper agate, agate-jasper, jaspagate

Primary Range

CHARACTERISTIC FEATURES:

- Irregular masses of opaque jasper intergrown with translucent chalcedony

- Small banded areas often exist between pieces of jasper

- Sometimes chalcedony bands and jasper alternate in vague layers

RARITY: Jasp-agates are fairly common—much more common than most collectors would like them to be

DESCRIPTION: Jasp-agates are a loosely defined variety of agate that contain banded chalcedony as well as masses of jasper. Like chalcedony, jasper is a variety of microcrystalline quartz, but unlike chalcedony, jasper consists of microscopic grains of quartz rather than fiber-like crystals. The primary visible difference between the two is that jasper lacks the translucency of chalcedony. It usually is opaque except in very thin sections. Since jasper and chalcedony are both varieties of quartz, it's not surprising that they can occur in the same specimen. When this unique interaction happens, jasp-agate specimens can have several distinct appearances. The most common type exhibits banded chalcedony, often white or gray in color, which weaves in between irregular masses of opaque

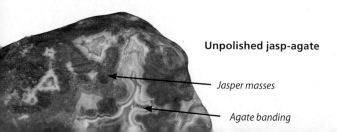

Unpolished jasp-agate

Jasper masses

Agate banding

53

red or brown jasper. The second, less common, type of jasp-agate is more perplexing and consists of twisting lace-like layers of chalcedony banded between layers of jasper, often with other softer minerals intergrown among them. This second type is technically not an agate, and must have originated from a process more sedimentary in nature than normal agates. Because of its agate banding, the first type is clearly the "truest" kind of jasp-agate and exemplifies this often-ignored variety of Lake Superior agate.

IDENTIFICATION: Jasp-agates have always been poorly defined, so it can be difficult to definitively label a specimen as a "jasp-agate." You'll simply have to rely on the presence of the two ingredients of jasp-agates: banded chalcedony and jasper. The banded chalcedony in most jasp-agates appears no different than in other agates, so its presence should be obvious. The masses of jasper, on the other hand, are most often very irregular and have no particular shape, though they are sometimes vaguely round in nature. In the more layered variety of jasp-agates, the jasper often has a more lace-like appearance with twisted and wavy boundaries between it and the next layer. In either type, the most important identifying trait to look for is jasper's opacity. Under a bright light, the difference between the chalcedony layers and jasper masses should be very apparent, as the chalcedony will allow some light through its surface while the jasper will not.

Polished jasp-agate

COLLECTIBILITY: To most Lake Superior agate collectors, jasp-agates are quickly relegated to the category of "ugly" or "junk" agates and are generally disregarded completely. Despite the fact that there certainly are some very attractive, colorful examples, they still are nearly valueless and few ever make their way into hobbyists' permanent collections. Polished specimens fare slightly better, however. With many imperfections and rough surfaces ground away in the polishing process, intricate details and interesting interactions between the jasper and chalcedony are often revealed. Under magnification, these can be more interesting to look at than many other varieties of Lake Superior agate.

Polished specimen

COMPARE & CONTRAST:

Moss Agate	Whorl Agate	Vein Agate	Fortification Agate
Contain tangles of hair-like inclusions	Contain wavy banding, but no opaque jasper	Banded structures are not within jasper	No jasper present

WHERE TO BEGIN LOOKING: Though jasp-agates are not particularly prominent in any single location, Ontario's Lake Superior shoreline, particularly along Nipigon Bay, has produced many specimens. The usual places—lakeshores, gravel pits and riverbeds—are all worth a look.

Polished agate with mineral inclusions

Embedded siderite crystals

Mineral Inclusions

SYNONYMS: None

Primary Range

CHARACTERISTIC FEATURES:

- Conspicuous solid masses or geometric shapes embedded in an agate
- Inclusions are often darkly colored, sometimes with a metallic luster, and can be softer than the rest of the agate
- Chalcedony banding often warps and bends around the masses to accommodate them

RARITY: Mineral inclusions are very common in Lake Superior agates, particularly in the Keweenaw Peninsula of Michigan, though they may not always be obvious

DESCRIPTION: Agates are not the only minerals that form in basalt and rhyolite vesicles (cavities); dozens of others can potentially grow within these rocks. So it should come as no surprise that various minerals, such as calcite, siderite, barite and zeolites, can be found intergrown within some agates. When this occurs, the minerals are called inclusions, and mineral inclusions are common in agates from all over the Lake Superior region. The inclusions are thought to have formed at the same time as the agate (or possibly earlier). As the agate filled in around the mineral crystals, the agate banding bent and contorted around them. Entombed in chalcedony, the inclusions survived so that we can enjoy their unique forms

**Polished agate with
mineral inclusion**

today. Not all mineral inclusions were so lucky, however. Some were dissolved and washed away by acidic water that later reached the agate. This process left crystal-shaped voids within the agate called crystal impressions (page 45), which are often categorized as a distinct type of mineral inclusion. Most mineral inclusions in Lake Superior agates are quite conspicuous, and they are often large and colored differently from the rest of the agate. But others are small and subtle and are often undetected by novices.

IDENTIFICATION: Most mineral inclusions in agates are obvious and easy to identify. That's because most inclusions clearly appear to be foreign to an agate's overall structure. In addition, the nearby chalcedony bands often warp and bend around the inclusions. When in doubt, bear in mind that the mineral inclusions are often whole crystals embedded in chalcedony and therefore exhibit distinct geometric shapes. Long, slender rectangles, jagged tooth-like points, and circular metallic masses are all examples of the kind of inclusions you may see embedded in a Lake Superior agate. In addition to these conspicuous shapes, the majority of mineral inclusions differ greatly in color from the rest of the agate. Inclusions that are very heavily stained with iron, for example, typically turn black. But despite the general ease of spotting mineral inclusions, there is a chance that you will come across some that are less obvious, and for those you may be able to test an inclusion's hardness. Any mineral inclusion will be softer than the agate that surrounds it. Calcite and barite, for example, will easily be scratched by a knife blade whereas chalcedony and quartz will not.

Barite mineral inclusions in polished agate

COLLECTIBILITY: Mineral inclusions may be common in Lake Superior agates, but from a collector's standpoint, they can "make or break" a specimen. If a mineral inclusion is well formed, it can enhance a specimen, making it quite desirable. On the other hand, if an inclusion mars the aesthetics of an agate's banding, it can make a specimen worthless. In the end, whether an agate with a mineral inclusion is collectible or not is largely a matter of a collector's personal preference.

Siderite inclusion

Circular hematite inclusions

COMPARE & CONTRAST:

Crystal Impressions	Tube Agate	Sagenitic Agate	Fragmented Membrane Agate
Geometric shapes are hollow	Channels that extend deep into the agate	Inclusions are in radial arrangements	Inclusions are discontinuous curved ribbons

WHERE TO BEGIN LOOKING: Gravel pits near Cloquet, Minnesota, and mine dumps on the Keweenaw Peninsula of Michigan often yield agates with abundant inclusions. The rare vein agates found near Thunder Bay, Ontario, also contain lots of mineral inclusions.

Exceptional, large unpolished paint agate

Common orange paint coloration

Macrocrystalline quartz

Paint Agate

SYNONYMS: Paint stones, painted agate, paints, opaque agate

CHARACTERISTIC FEATURES:
- The majority of bands are opaque and typically exhibit brown, orange, pink, tan and white coloration
- Paint coloration can be present in agates with any banding structure (such as fortification and water-level agates), and in any agate with inclusions, including agates with sagenitic growths
- Many paint agates can be found still embedded in their host rock

RARITY: Small paint agates and paint agates still embedded in their host rock are not uncommon, but very vividly colored specimens or those larger than your fist are quite rare; paint agates are more common in Minnesota

DESCRIPTION: With stones as hard and durable as Lake Superior agates, it's easy to think of them as being impervious to the elements. But agates are just the product of chemical reactions, and they are subject to additional chemical changes. In most agates, exposure to acidic water, air and sunlight has altered and changed their coloration to the translucent reds, browns and grays Lake Superior agate collectors recognize. But those agates didn't originally form in those hues. Agates embedded

Polished paint agate

in their host rock have a higher concentration of unweathered iron mineral impurities within their chalcedony than agates found on beaches or in gravel pits. The result is iron-rich shades of intense orange, deep brown, pale tans, and even soft pink, all of which are opaque and allow very little light to pass through them, like layers of paint. Some agates found free of their matrix can also exhibit paint coloration, but these examples simply haven't yet been exposed to enough weathering.

IDENTIFICATION: As with any color variation, paint coloration can be found in almost any structural variety of agate, with fortification agates (page 23) and floater agates (page 49) most commonly exhibiting the opaque paint agate hues. Less commonly, water-level agates (page 35) and agates with prominent inclusions, such as sagenitic agates (page 103) can also exhibit paint coloration. Whatever a specimen's classification, identifying whether or not it displays paint coloration is very easy. Color is often the initial clue, as most paint agates occur in various shades of orange. Most agates that have undergone sufficient weathering no longer contain such vivid oranges, which have instead turned into deep reds and browns over time. But orange isn't the only color present in paint agates, so you'll have to rely on the most diagnostic trait: opacity. Paint agates get their name because their colored banding is opaque, and appears to be painted onto the surface of the stone. In all other agates, the colored chalcedony bands, no matter how dark, are translucent.

Exceptional polished paint agate

COLLECTIBILITY: When it comes to the collectibility of Lake Superior agates, fortification agates (page 23) may exceed all others, but paint agates are a very close runner-up. In fact, very well-formed fortification agates with paint coloration are among the most valuable Lake Superior agates, especially when free of fractures and other distracting damage. Of course, a specimen's value depends on its quality, and the most desirable specimens have the common vivid orange coloration contrasting with many broad white or gray bands. Pale paint agates that appear pink are also valuable, but these are exceptionally rare.

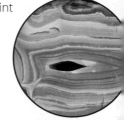

Paint agate with smoky quartz

Paint agate embedded in basalt

COMPARE & CONTRAST:

Rare Colorations	Colored Macrocrystalline Quartz	Surface Colorations
Uncommon coloration	Quartz crystals, not chalcedony bands, are uniquely colored	Odd coloration is only on outer surfaces

WHERE TO BEGIN LOOKING: Fantastic specimens are found in gravel pits and along Lake Superior's shoreline in Grand Marais, Minnesota, as well as in road cuts and riverbeds at the far northern end of the Keweenaw Peninsula, near Copper Harbor, Michigan

Exceptional unpolished tube agate

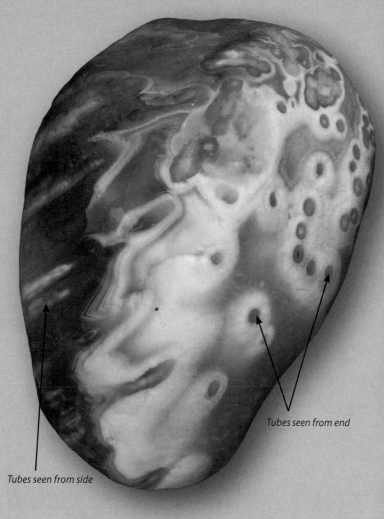

Tubes seen from end

Tubes seen from side

Tube Agate

SYNONYMS: None

Primary Range

CHARACTERISTIC FEATURES:

- Long, slender, tube- or tunnel-like growths that extend from one side of an agate all the way to the other, with distinct circular markings that can often be seen on each side

- Tubes can occasionally be hollow or banded, or both

- Tubes are typically parallel and straight, rarely changing direction, often giving one side of a specimen the appearance of containing many circular dots or "eyes"

- Chalcedony bands often warp and bend to accommodate the tubes

RARITY: Tube agates are fairly common throughout the Lake Superior region, but agates with hollow or well-banded tubes are much rarer

DESCRIPTION: Like stalactitic agates (page 107), the structures in tube agates are the result of chalcedony clinging to needle-like crystals of other minerals as the agate formed. Tube agates are named for the way these long, slender structures appear to tunnel their way through an agate. But the name isn't apt for every specimen; thanks to weathering, the minerals that originally made the elongated structures have worn away in some specimens, leaving hollow

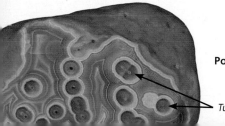

Polished tube agate

Tubes

tubes that extend through the agate. The tubes don't often stay hollow for long, however, as later influxes of silica can fill them with quartz. This produces agates that appear to contain long streaks of color from some angles, while only the circular tops and bottoms of the tubes can be observed from others.

IDENTIFICATION: Any veteran collector will be able to quickly spot the telltale signs of a tube agate because they are incredibly distinctive once you've seen enough examples. One of their most prominent traits is the way the elongated tubes grow more or less parallel to each other, which gives specimens a "streaky" appearance that instantly distinguishes them from sagenitic agates (page 103). You're more likely to confuse tube agates with stalactitic agates (page 107), which are nearly identical except that stalactitic agates' elongated structures only extend partway into the agate. In tube agates, however, the tubes begin on one surface of an agate and continue through to the other side, creating circular eye-like structures on each surface. These in turn can then be confused with eye agates (page 83), but eyes are actually hemispheres and don't extend through an agate.

COLLECTIBILITY: Tube agates are one of the most common varieties of Lake Superior agates that contain inclusions, and, as most collectors dislike agates with abundant inclusions, most tube agates are ignored as a result. But like sagenitic agates (page 103), when a

Unpolished tubes within macrocrystalline quartz

particularly beautiful, well-formed example turns up, tube agates have the ability to occasionally excite collectors. Though they are not worth as much as fortification agates (page 23), specimens with many large tubes ringed with colorful bands can be very desirable. And for the casual collector, specimens with ample translucent quartz allow the length of the tubes to be observed deep within the agate, which can make a specimen very intriguing, albeit not particularly valuable.

Banded tubes

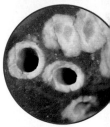

Hollow tubes

COMPARE & CONTRAST:

Stalactitic Agate	Eye Agate	Moss Agate	Sagenitic Agate
Icicle-like structures that extend partway through an agate	Circular structures that do not extend deep into the agate	Plentiful tangles of hair-like inclusions	Inclusions are in radial arrangements

WHERE TO BEGIN LOOKING: Tube agates are common along Lake Superior's shore in Minnesota, Ontario and Michigan, as well as in gravel pits near Duluth and Cloquet, Minnesota.

Uncommon

Many of Lake Superior's agate varieties take some effort to find, but the results are spectacular

Many of the most popular and most interesting varieties of Lake Superior agates are quite uncommon. This includes agates with odd variations in structure, those that have been uniquely weathered, and agates with rare inclusions, all of which can be found sparingly around the region.

Brecciated Agate
(pg. 71)

**Colored Macrocrystal-
line Quartz** (pg. 75)

Dendritic Agate
(pg. 79)

Eye Agate
(pg. 83)

Faulted Agate
(pg. 87)

**Fragmented Membrane
Agate** (pg. 91)

Agate Geode
(pg. 95)

Peeled Agate
(pg. 99)

Sagenitic Agate
(pg. 103)

Stalactitic Agate
(pg. 107)

Vein Agate
(pg. 111)

**Water-washed
Agate** (pg. 115)

Polished brecciated agate

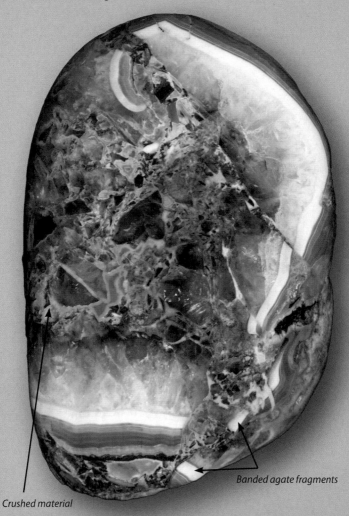

Crushed material

Banded agate fragments

Primary Range

Brecciated Agate

SYNONYMS: Ruin agate, agate breccia, crushed agate, debris agate

CHARACTERISTIC FEATURES:

- Masses of chalcedony and quartz that contain numerous irregular fragments of a broken banded agate

- Pieces of agate banding are often "mismatched" and individual bands don't line up well

- Fragments of agate are typically cemented together by colorless quartz crystals, chalcedony, or opaque chert and jasper

RARITY: Broken and fragmented agates are uncommon, but very fine examples of brecciated agate are considerably more rare

DESCRIPTION: In geology, the term "breccia" refers to rocks that consist of broken, angular fragments of stone that have been cemented together by a fine-grained material. Brecciated agates match this definition exactly, though they are much more interesting than any brecciated rock. In one of the most unique examples of agate weathering, brecciated agates were crushed at some point in their existence, but the resulting pieces were not completely scattered. In fact, there is significant evidence that many brecciated agates were broken while still embedded in their original vesicle (cavity) and

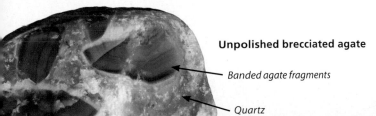

Unpolished brecciated agate

Banded agate fragments

Quartz

retain nearly all of their original material. However, some brecciated agates were clearly free of their matrix when they shattered. In either case, before these agates' fragments were lost, silica solutions flowed in between the pieces and crystallized, cementing them into a continuous mass once more. The silica cement frequently takes the form of granular quartz, but can also be chert or jasper, depending on the environment in which the agate was broken. This results in specimens with banded agate fragments that are misplaced and resemble pieces of a puzzle.

IDENTIFICATION: Brecciated agates are not common, and most collectors won't ever find a particularly fine example. Some of the best specimens still retain an agate-like shape and contain a shell of more or less intact banding surrounding a mass of crushed chalcedony and quartz fragments. But those specimens are easy to identify because they have so much in common with normal, unbroken agates. On the other hand, brecciated agates consisting of disordered agate fragments suspended in a mass of chert or quartz can be harder to identify. Layered jasper can sometimes be found in a similar state, so look for the distinctive translucency of chalcedony combined with bands that follow the shape of the fragments. If a specimen appears only lightly brecciated, it's probably actually a faulted agate (page 87). Faulted agates weren't as unlucky as brecciated agates and were merely cracked and shifted, rather than being crushed entirely.

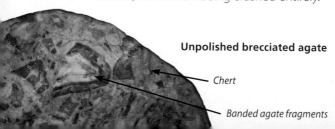

Unpolished brecciated agate

Chert

Banded agate fragments

COLLECTIBILITY: Given that serious Lake Superior agate collectors often scrutinize every specimen for even the tiniest flaws, it may come as a surprise that brecciated agates can be very collectible. Perhaps it's because of the incredible detail in each specimen or speculation about why they were damaged, but brecciated agates capture the attention and admiration of most collectors, though that doesn't necessarily mean that they are valuable. In the most desirable specimens, there are many visible large banded fragments and it's clear that the original material was a whole agate. Bright coloration and the addition of rare features, such as amethyst (page 75), help make a specimen more valuable as well.

Unpolished brecciated agate

Specimen courtesy of David Gredzens

COMPARE & CONTRAST:

Faulted Agate

Exhibit "healed" cracks

WHERE TO BEGIN LOOKING: Look for brecciated agates in areas that saw greater volcanic activity, such as the entire shoreline of Lake Superior in Minnesota, and on the Keweenaw Peninsula north of Houghton, Michigan.

Polished agate with colored quartz

Greenish smoky quartz

Normally colored macrocrystalline quartz

Colored Macrocrystalline Quartz

SYNONYMS: Amethyst; citrine; smoky quartz, Morion quartz; Cairngorm quartz, root beer quartz

Primary Range

CHARACTERISTIC FEATURES:
- An agate with coarse crystals of colored quartz, often at the center of an agate or surrounding portions of chalcedony banding
- Colors include purple, gray, black, yellow, brown or green
- Colored quartz can often exist alongside common white or colorless quartz crystals

RARITY: Particular quartz colorations have specific names; agates with gray (smoky quartz) and purple (amethyst) quartz are uncommon, while yellow (citrine), dark brown (Cairngorm quartz), black (Morion quartz), or green quartz is very rare in Lake Superior agates

DESCRIPTION: As most Lake Superior agates are over one billion years old, they've endured a variety of natural forces—everything from earthquakes and volcanoes to immense glaciers and millennia of weathering. Each of these forces can impact a stone in specific ways. Most of the time, seismic activity crushes an agate, or chemical solutions stain the chalcedony various colors. But when the invisible force of radioactivity is involved, the results can be spectacular. Tiny amounts of impurities—particularly iron and aluminum—are often present within the crystals of macrocrystalline

Polished agate with colored quartz

Cairngorm (brown) quartz

75

quartz in many agates. When radiation contacts impure quartz crystals, it excites the iron and aluminum atoms, causing them to vibrate. (Such radiation is released from minerals and water deep within the earth.) The vibrations generate color within the crystals until some other energy source, such as heat, causes the atoms to cease moving. In Lake Superior agates, gray quartz (called smoky quartz) is common and caused by aluminum impurities, while purple quartz (called amethyst) is caused by iron atoms vibrating. Somewhat strangely, the chalcedony bands in affected agates are unchanged.

IDENTIFICATION: Generally speaking, the presence of macrocrystalline quartz in an agate is obvious, but when it's colored, it is even more apparent. But that doesn't mean you can't get confused when trying to identify an agate's colored quartz. Purple amethyst is fairly unmistakable and gray smoky quartz and black Morion quartz are easily identified as well, but yellow citrine and brown Cairngorm quartz (also called root beer quartz) are another matter. Yellow and brown quartz are seemingly common in the Lake Superior region due to the prevalent iron minerals that often stain quartz, but colored quartz and stained quartz are not the same. When identifying any colored quartz, use magnification to determine whether the color is part of the quartz or actually the result of many tiny, finely dispersed grains of impurities staining the surface of the crystals. Yellow "citrine" in most agates is actually caused by tiny grainy flecks of goethite.

Unpolished agate with colored quartz

Amethyst

COLLECTIBILITY: Colored macrocrystalline quartz can make even the most mundane Lake Superior agate considerably more collectible, and even valuable if the coloration of the quartz is vivid enough. Professional collectors and novices alike appreciate colored quartz in agates both for its rarity and beauty, but not all colors are equally desirable. Gray smoky quartz is uncommon but often uninteresting, especially if pale, while purple (amethyst), one of the more common colorations in the Lake Superior region, is extremely desirable no matter its shade. Yellow citrine is prized for its rarity, as is brown Cairngorm quartz and black Morion quartz, all three of which occur so infrequently in Lake Superior agates that even poor specimens are coveted by collectors.

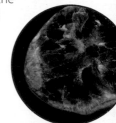

Morion quartz

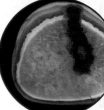

Citrine in agate

COMPARE & CONTRAST:

Banded Quartz Agate	Rare Colorations	Skip-an-Atom Agate
Quartz is typically white or colorless	Chalcedony, not quartz, is uniquely colored	Quartz is opaque and bluish gray

WHERE TO BEGIN LOOKING: Agates with colored quartz are widespread but not abundant. Amethyst-bearing agates tend to be more common along Minnesota's shoreline north of Grand Marais, extending to the shores east of Thunder Bay.

Polished agate with unusually large dendrite (approx. 1")

Dendrites between layers

Dendritic Agate

SYNONYMS: Dendrites

Primary Range

CHARACTERISTIC FEATURES:
- Small, tree- or fern-like growths within an agate, often on the surfaces of interior bands
- Dendrites are extraordinarily thin and are nearly two-dimensional,
- Dendrites in Lake Superior agates are typically only reddish orange or yellow

RARITY: Dendrites in agates are more common than most collectors think; however, dendrites are typically very small and only easily visible when polished or very well formed

DESCRIPTION: Of all the many mineral inclusions that can be found in Lake Superior agates, dendrites are often the most intricate and fascinating. Dendrites derive their name from the Greek word for "tree-like," and well-formed dendrites do indeed resemble trees or ferns in shape. When one or more dendrites are present in an agate, the agate is known as a dendritic agate. Most dendrites in agates are quite small—less than a quarter of an inch—sometimes too small to be easily noticed in an unpolished agate. But rare examples can be up to an inch long, and in these specimens the fine, delicate details of dendrites can be appreciated. How they formed is as interesting

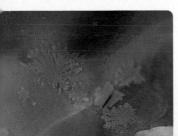

Dendrite (approx. ¼") on surface of peeled agate

as the dendrites themselves: agates are not as solid as they may seem and there are microscopic spaces between the bands where water can collect. As iron-rich groundwater seeps into these spaces, tiny particles of iron minerals, such as hematite and goethite, are free to move randomly through the water. When two particles contact each other, they bond, and then catch more free-moving particles. Eventually, when enough iron particles have built upon each other, a visible dendrite appears deep between agate bands.

IDENTIFICATION: Most dendrites are very small, making them difficult to spot in agates. This means that they are not quite as rare as they initially may seem; they're just too small to notice. They can occur between the bands of virtually any agate type, so every specimen is worthy of a search for dendrites. A microscope or loupe will be essential for finding and identifying them, but to give yourself the best chance of finding a dendrite, look in polished agates. It's often impossible see the fine details deep within an unpolished agate and any dendrites will likely be obscured. Unpolished peeled agates are the exception (page 99); in these stones, some of the agate layers have actually separated to reveal the surfaces of interior bands. Because this is where dendrites in agates form, you may get lucky and find a dendrite exposed on a smooth, peeled surface. The only other type of inclusion you may confuse with a dendrite is a plume (page 125), but while dendrites are microscopically thin and are essentially two-dimensional, plumes have depth and extend deeper into the agate.

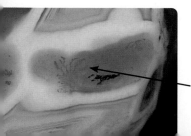

Dendrite (approx. ⅛") within polished agate

COLLECTIBILITY: Dendritic agates catch the attention of many collectors, but only when they contain a large, well-formed and easily visible dendrite. Since the vast majority of dendrites are too small to appreciate without magnification, they typically do not have a bearing on an agate's value. In fact, most collectors may not even realize that they have dendritic agates in their collection until they closely examine their specimens under a microscope. But those rare, awe-inspiring dendrites with exquisitely detailed branches delight collectors and can increase an otherwise mundane agate specimen's value considerably.

Dendrite

COMPARE & CONTRAST:

Plume Agate

Plant-like structures are not flat

Mineral Inclusions

Inclusions are not plant-like in structure

WHERE TO BEGIN LOOKING: There are no sites where dendrites are consistently found, so you can start your search anywhere. Since they are sometimes found on peeled agates, try looking in gravel pits near Duluth, Minnesota, and in northern Wisconsin, where peeled agates often turn up.

Polished eye agate with unusual coloration

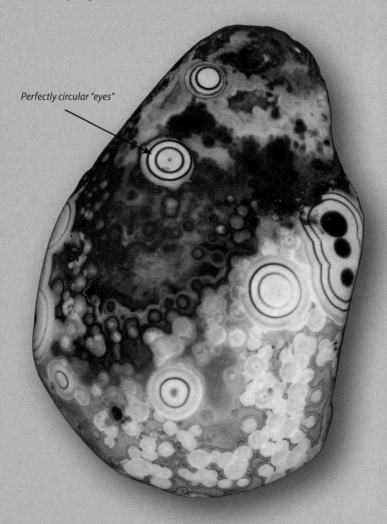

Perfectly circular "eyes"

Eye Agate

Primary Range

SYNONYMS: Fish-eye agate, bull's-eye agate, hemisphere agate

CHARACTERISTIC FEATURES:
- Nearly perfectly circular spots on the outer surfaces of agates, particularly on small specimens
- Circular "eyes" are often banded with bull's-eye-like rings
- Agate eyes are hemispheres that do not extend far into the agate

RARITY: Eye agates aren't particularly rare; however, many eyes on agates are quite small and easily overlooked, making eye agates seem more uncommon than they actually are

DESCRIPTION: A favorite among collectors, eye agates obviously derive their name from the perfectly circular spots, or "eyes," on their outer surfaces. These eye-like circles are typically only found on the exterior of an agate and formed when the tiny chalcedony spherulites that make up the agate's outer husk (see page 12) continued to grow outward. These seemingly two-dimensional shapes are actually hemispheres, or half spheres, which extend inward like a bowl. Nevertheless, they do not extend far into an agate, so if an eye agate becomes too weathered or is too aggressively polished, the eyes will disappear altogether. While

Unpolished eye agate

the most popular specimens exhibit eyes with multiple bull's-eye-like rings, most agate eyes contain only a central spot of color surrounded by a wide band of another color. Others may be completely blank or filled in with a solid color. And though large isolated eyes may be as striking as they are endearing, specimens exhibiting masses of many tiny intergrown eyes are more abundant. The eyes on these specimens appear like many bubbles on the surface of water. In any specimen, tiny eyes can be hard to spot.

IDENTIFICATION: Eyes on an agate are normally obvious and easily identified by sight alone. The eye agate's nearly perfectly circular banded spots are hard to miss, especially when pea-sized or larger. But eyes are not the only circular features that can be found on an agate, and it's surprising how many collectors misidentify other round structures as "eyes." Likely due to the popularity of the eye agate, tube agates (page 65), stalactitic agates (page 107), and even fortification agates that have circular patterns in their banding are frequently confused for eye agates and are often mislabeled as such. Therefore, it's important to be able to recognize the primary characteristics of the eye agate. First, remember that eyes are surface features and are therefore only found on the exterior of a specimen. Large circular formations deep within the pattern of an agate are not eyes, but simply round banded areas. Secondly, remember that agate eyes are hemispheres, which means that even large eyes extend only partway into the agate. This can help differentiate them from

Polished eye agate

Eye with multiple bands

tube and stalactitic agates, which have circular features that extend deeply into the agate, sometimes all the way through it.

COLLECTIBILITY: Eye agates have always been one of the most popular varieties of Lake Superior agate, and likely always will be. Novices and experienced collectors alike find the eyes endearing and every hobbyist has a prized eye agate. While they are not very rare, eye agates with large, well-formed eyes can command relatively high prices, even when the specimens themselves are quite small. The most sought-after specimens have coin-sized eyes, or eyes with many high-contrast red and white bands, but none reach the lofty values of fine fortification agates.

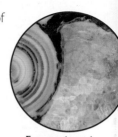

Eye agate cut perpendicular to eye structure

Polished eye agate

COMPARE & CONTRAST:

Tube Agate	Sagenitic Agate	Whorl Agate

Circular shapes extend deep into the specimen

Circular formations are formed of needles

Patterns are not perfectly circular

WHERE TO BEGIN LOOKING: Most agates with eyes are small, and the high volume of small water-worn agates on Lake Superior's beaches makes them a great place to start. Brockway Mountain on the Keweenaw Peninsula in Michigan and gravel pits near Grand Marais, Minnesota, are also good places to look.

Polished faulted agate

Macrocrystalline quartz

Faulted, misaligned banding

Faulted Agate

SYNONYMS: Ruin agate

Primary Range

CHARACTERISTIC FEATURES:

- Banding that appears misaligned and disjointed due to cracks and other visible physical damage to an agate

- Fragments of banding are typically not missing, but only "misplaced"

- Broken banding is cemented together by quartz or chalcedony, often of a different color than the rest of the agate

RARITY: Faulted agates are uncommon throughout the Lake Superior region, but are slightly more abundant in the Keweenaw Peninsula of Michigan

DESCRIPTION: At over one billion years old, Lake Superior agates have endured a great deal of weathering, and almost no agate has survived unscathed. Nearly all agates have chips and fractures caused by the glaciers, but that damage is very recent compared to the seismic activity they endured when they were first forming. Agates are thought to have developed soon after the volcanic rock in which they formed, making them liable to the volcanic activity— including earthquakes—that produced the host rock. This shifted the rock around the agates, sometimes crushing them. Faulted agates were created when an agate was

Polished faulted agate

Large quartz-filled crack

87

cracked by the moving rock, which subsequently shifted the agate banding. This gives faulted agates unique sections of mismatched banding, called faults, where the bands don't line up correctly. Sometimes the banding is completely segmented and shifted in several places, like a jigsaw puzzle missing pieces, but most of the time it's a single crack that caused the misalignment of the bands. Later, the cracks were healed shut by additional quartz. This process is nearly identical to the formation of brecciated agates (page 71), but it occurred to a lesser degree in faulted agates.

IDENTIFICATION: Since you can find multiple cracks and fractures in nearly every Lake Superior agate, it may initially seem like faulted agates are common. On the contrary, agates with shifted banding are quite uncommon because the vast majority of damage to agates occurred after the agate was freed from its host rock. In addition, the sheer volume of agates with significant fractures makes finding one with a fault a bit like looking for a needle in a haystack. To find a fault, carefully study and observe your specimens, especially polished examples in which faults are easier to see. When you've identified a fracture larger than most, and one that appears to be "healed" together, follow its length, and carefully look for shifted bands. If you find what appears to be an agate with many severe faults, it's most likely a brecciated agate (page 71). Brecciated agates formed by a similar, but more violent, process.

Unpolished faulted agate

Specimen courtesy of Terry and Bobbi House

COLLECTIBILITY: Like their battered cousins, brecciated agates, faulted agates are surprisingly collectible, considering that they are "ruined" specimens. Though they are often viewed more as a curiosity than an investment, colorful specimens with fine cracks and noticeably shifted banding can still be quite valuable. The Keweenaw Peninsula of Michigan is particularly well known for faulted agates, sometimes with so many iron-stained cracks that they become more prominent than the agate banding. But not all examples are desirable, and many faulted agates contain dark impurity-stained quartz, obscuring an agate's bands and making it nearly worthless.

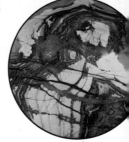

Paint agate with multiple faults

COMPARE & CONTRAST:

Brecciated Agate

Agates are crushed and "healed" back together

WHERE TO BEGIN LOOKING: Like brecciated agates, look in areas that saw greater volcanic activity, such as Lake Superior's entire shore in Minnesota, Ontario's Nipigon Bay area, and especially the Keweenaw Peninsula north of Houghton, Michigan.

Polished fragmented membrane agate

Banded pattern

Membrane fragments

Fragmented Membrane Agate

Primary Range

SYNONYMS: Membrane agate

CHARACTERISTIC FEATURES:

- Areas of chalcedony containing thin, curving, ribbon-like fragments of a soft, opaque mineral embedded in the agate

- The fragments are often pitted and hollowed

- Chalcedony banding is typically confined to a fragment-free region of the agate

RARITY: Fragmented membrane agates are uncommon and can occasionally be found anywhere in the Lake Superior region

DESCRIPTION: When a vesicle (cavity) forms within basalt or other volcanic rock, the volatile gases and water trapped within it begin to interact with the surrounding rock, creating new minerals in the process. This is the source of the chlorite or celadonite membrane (page 13) that lines countless vesicles in the Lake Superior region and coats virtually every agate freshly removed from its host rock. But what would happen if that membrane were to fall into an agate that was forming? Fragmented membrane agates answer that question. They contain numerous curving, ribbon-like fragments of the minerals that originally lined the cavity; in fragmented membrane agates, these remnants are suspended in chalcedony. The fragments are typically separated into a lower portion of the

**Polished fragmented
membrane agate**

91

agate that does not contain any banding, which signifies that they peeled off the vesicle walls and sank into the water-filled vesicle before the agate had formed. The fragments also almost always appear curved or with curled ends, which is thought to occur due to tension within the structure of each fragment. But remember that these fragments were originally made of green chlorite or celadonite, both of which are extremely soft minerals. As a result, weathering has affected the fragments, staining them red or brown with iron and causing them to be partially worn away and pitted.

IDENTIFICATION: Even in rough, unpolished specimens, the soft, curled membrane fragments are generally very obvious and instantly recognizable, though they are best appreciated in polished specimens. Still, even novice collectors should be able to easily identify fragmented membrane agates. The only difficulty arises when a specimen is heavily weathered or damaged, in which case the specimen may appear to be a moss agate (page 27). Moss agates, however, typically contain many more inclusions and little to no chalcedony banding. Another characteristic trait of fragmented membrane agates is that one side of each ribbon-like piece appears rougher and more uneven than the other. The smoother side is thought to have originally adhered to the vesicle's inner wall.

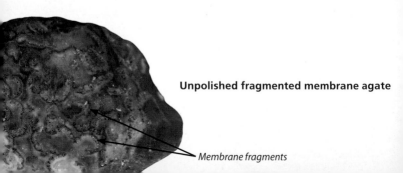

Unpolished fragmented membrane agate

Membrane fragments

COLLECTIBILITY: As a general rule, with Lake Superior agates, the more inclusions an agate has, the less desirable it becomes to serious collectors. The many inclusions in fragmented membrane agates give specimens a "messy" appearance that most veteran collectors find off-putting. These agates still have their advocates, however, and fragmented membrane agates appeal to certain collectors who value "weird" agates or those with unique inclusions. But while some specimens certainly are beautiful, these agates are typically ignored and hold relatively little value. In addition, since the membrane fragments consist primarily of softer minerals, specimens will often exhibit pits and holes where weathering has affected them.

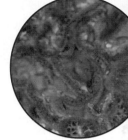

Close-up of fragments

Polishing these agates creates a similar effect, as the fragments wear away, leaving the polished surfaces of a specimen pitted, uneven and littered with unattractive dull spots.

COMPARE & CONTRAST:

Moss Agate

Inclusions are very fine, branching tube structures

Tube Agate

Inclusions are less plentiful and are tube-like

WHERE TO BEGIN LOOKING: While these agates can be found almost anywhere in the region, gravel pits near Duluth, Minnesota, have produced large and fine examples.

Unpolished agate geode

Hollow center

Agate Geode

SYNONYMS: Geode

Primary Range

CHARACTERISTIC FEATURES:
- A hollow cavity at the center of an agate's pattern
- Lake Superior agate geodes typically have fortification banding or water-level banding
- The central cavity can contain mineral growths, such as tiny quartz crystals, zeolite crystals, and calcite crystals or masses

RARITY: Lake Superior agate geodes are uncommon due to their unique formation and fragile nature; agate geodes still embedded in their host rock may be more common as they are more protected from weathering

DESCRIPTION: There are many types of geodes throughout the world, but all have the same defining feature: their centers are hollow. Agate geodes are no exception, though they are quite uncommon in the Lake Superior region. In agate geodes, a shell of banded chalcedony encloses the void at its center, though the thickness of the chalcedony layers can vary greatly. Many thick-walled agate geodes are found in the Lake Superior region, presumably because they are less fragile than their thin-walled counterparts, which were easily crushed by the glaciers. It's easy to understand how the hollow

Agate geode embedded in rhyolite

Large calcite crystal
Laumontite (orange)
Agate banding
Specimen courtesy of Christopher Cordes

95

centers of geodes form once one understands that agates form from their outer layers inward. During formation, the supply of silica to the agate was interrupted and never replenished; therefore, agate geodes are actually "unfinished" agates. But when it comes to agate geodes, it's what is inside the cavity that is most interesting. Most are lined with tiny quartz crystal points, but others contain more exciting mineral growths, such as zeolites and calcite.

IDENTIFICATION: Agate geodes may be the easiest of all Lake Superior agates to identify—just look for a cavity at the center of an agate. Whether it is large enough to be the dominant feature of a specimen or too small to hold a pea, the void is the key identifying feature. Typically, geode centers are found in fortification agates (page 23), but more rarely they can also be found in water-level agates (page 35). Identifying the various minerals found growing at the center of an agate geode is an entirely different matter. Most of the time, only a thin crust of tiny quartz crystal points will be found lining the interior of the cavity—this is called a quartz druse. Less common minerals attract more attention. Soft white calcite, blocky orange laumontite, and delicate needles of thomsonite are all minerals that can rarely be found crystallized within Lake Superior agate geodes. Finally, novices should be careful not to confuse agate geodes with crystal impressions (page 45), which are geometrically shaped cavities that formed when crystals of other minerals dissolved.

Polished agate geode

Quartz druse

COLLECTIBILITY: Agate geodes are quite collectible, especially if the cavity adds to the aesthetics and beauty of a specimen. But while many serious collectors will have a few Lake Superior agate geodes in their collection, it is the unique mineral crystals sometimes found inside them that are the real draw. Mineral growths in agate geodes are not rare throughout the world, but they are extremely uncommon in the Lake Superior region, making specimens that contain well-formed crystals of any mineral highly desirable.

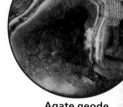

Agate geode

COMPARE & CONTRAST:

Fortification Agate	Crystal Impressions	Tube Agate
Similar banding, but no hollow center	Geometric, angular cavities, not necessarily in the center	Hollow channels that extend through the agate

WHERE TO BEGIN LOOKING: Some of the most interesting geodes are still embedded in basalt near Lake Superior's shore around Grand Marais, Minnesota. The majority of specimens, however, come from gravel pits near Duluth.

Unpolished peeled agate

Large, flat, peeled area

Common agate banding

Peeled Agate

Primary Range

SYNONYMS: Peeler

CHARACTERISTIC FEATURES:

- The exterior of the agate has smooth, solid-colored portions that are broad and curving
- Smooth surfaces are parallel to interior agate bands
- Smooth surfaces themselves are not banded

RARITY: Peeled agates are not rare in the region, but very fine examples with large peels are uncommon and typically only come from gravel pits

DESCRIPTION: There are many ways that an agate can weather and break down, but one unique way Lake Superior agates erode is called peeling. This happens because agates are not quite as compact and solid as they seem. There are microscopic spaces between an agate's bands that are virtually invisible, even under very powerful microscopes. But they do exist, and the pervasive nature of water means that it can easily seep through the microscopic pores in an agate and collect in these miniscule spaces. When the water freezes and expands, the tiny spaces between bands can widen slightly. After years of freezing, thawing and other forms of weathering, the spaces between the layers can be widened enough that the upper layers

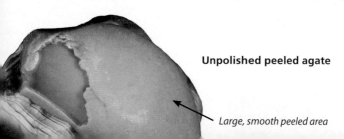

Unpolished peeled agate

Large, smooth peeled area

99

of an agate break off. The result is an agate with smooth, curving outer surfaces that are aligned parallel to the banded pattern. To help visualize this, think of cutting an onion in half. When you do, you see its many rings in cross-section. But if you peel the outer layers of an onion off of the inner layers, you do not see the rings but instead reveal another smooth layer of the onion. This is the same principle at work in peeled agates.

IDENTIFICATION: Identifying whether or not your agate is a peeled agate is as simple as observing the outer textures of the specimen. Most agates, even ones worn smooth by the glaciers or well-rounded by rivers, will exhibit a bumpy and slightly rough, irregular texture. Peeled sections of agates are always very smooth and even, often with a very waxy feel. At most, they can occasionally exhibit tiny circular impressions. In addition, the peeled surfaces of an agate are always evenly colored and show little to know variation, as they are the sides of individual interior bands. And though peels can occur on any variety of agate, they are most common on fortification agates (page 23) or water-level agates (page 35). As if peeled agates weren't interesting enough, the peeled surfaces are often home to dendrites (page 79). Because dendrites form at the point of weakness at which agates can peel, they are sometimes revealed when the layers of an agate separate.

COLLECTIBILITY: Lake Superior agate collectors know peeled agates better as "peelers," and though they are fairly common and interesting, their

Unpolished peeled agate

Large peeled area

collectibility is quite limited. Of course, this depends greatly on an individual collector's taste. Some collectors love the smooth, sweeping curves of heavily peeled agates while others feel that they are distracting unless they add to the beauty of a specimen or reveal interesting features not normally seen in an unpeeled agate. In either case, peelers generally hold lower values than their unweathered counterparts. Typically, the peeled agates that are the least valuable are those with large peeled surfaces but very little exposed banding.

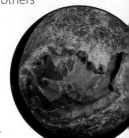

Whole agate with small peeled area

COMPARE & CONTRAST:

Ventifacts	**Water-washed Agate**	**Brecciated Agate**
Brightly lustrous and pitted	Smooth and rounded on all sides	Agates that are crushed and "healed" back together

WHERE TO BEGIN LOOKING: Gravel pits and riverbeds near Duluth and Two Harbors, Minnesota, are good places to start looking for peelers, as is the area around Superior, Wisconsin.

Polished sagenitic agate

Radially arranged needle-like crystals

Circular color zones

Sagenitic Agate

SYNONYMS: Sagenite

Primary Range

CHARACTERISTIC FEATURES:

- Circular arrangements of thin, slender, needle-like structures, often with distinct rings of color

- Sagenitic structures can appear complete and circular, but often are only a semi-circular "spray" of needles

- Sagenitic agates often lack common agate banding

- The needle-like structures can sometimes be visibly hollow

RARITY: Sagenitic agates are uncommon throughout the Lake Superior region, but very well-formed and colorful examples are rare and typically found in Minnesota

DESCRIPTION: Known better among Lake Superior agate collectors as "sagenites," sagenitic agates are one of the most sought-after varieties of inclusion-bearing agates. These incredibly unique agates typically contain little to no common agate banding and instead exhibit radial arrangements, or "sprays," of long needle-like structures, often with circular zones of color. These shapes are actually the remnants of minerals of the zeolite group, specifically thomsonite, natrolite and mesolite. Not coincidentally, these minerals grow as delicate needle-like crystals typically arranged into radial structures. Zeolites also form almost exclusively from the decomposition

Unpolished sagenitic agate

of basalt, so it should come as no surprise that they often formed within a vesicle at the same time it was filled with silica. Later, as the silica hardened into chalcedony, the zeolite mineral formations were entombed, eventually becoming sagenitic agates. The shapes exhibited by sagenitic agates are sometimes completely circular, but are most often semi-circular, and can be of any color. Opacity can differ between specimens, but the needle-like structures are typically opaque and the chalcedony between them is translucent.

IDENTIFICATION: Sagenite formations are a unique variety of mineral inclusion, so the same tricks used to identify other agates with inclusions can be used for sagenitic agates. Actually, thanks to the spectacular growths of the embedded zeolite minerals, sagenitic agates are easier to identify than most other inclusions. But due to the similar shapes found in eye agates (page 83), many novices confuse the two, so it is important to learn the differences. When examining a specimen, first look for needle-like structures; these are common in sagenite formations but not present in eye agates. Upon close inspection (preferably under magnification) many of the needles will look weathered and the zeolite minerals that formed them are absent, making them resemble many tiny hollow tubes. Also, sagenite formations are often lopsided, whereas agate eyes are almost always perfectly circular. Finally, agate eyes are shallow surface features while many sagenite structures are large enough to extend through an entire specimen.

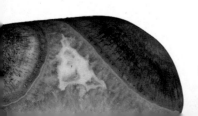

Polished sagenitic agate

COLLECTIBILITY: Of all the varieties of Lake Superior agates containing inclusions, sagenitic agates are without question the most popular. Even most traditional agate collectors who primarily value banded agates can appreciate a well-formed sagenite. The most desirable and valuable specimens contain either a single, large sagenite formation that fills most of an agate or one with several well-defined smaller formations around an agate's perimeter. In either case, color is key. The more vivid the coloration, the better, especially if the sagenitic forms contain multiple bands. In short, if a specimen displays a large, attractive sagenite "spray," its value can soar above that of any other agate with inclusions.

Circular sagenite

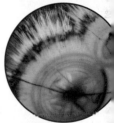

Thomsonite specimen for comparison

COMPARE & CONTRAST:

Eye Agate	Mineral Inclusions	Whorl Agate
Contain small, perfectly circular spots	Inclusions are not in radial arrangements	Circular structures are not composed of needles

WHERE TO BEGIN LOOKING: Sagenitic agates are found primarily in Minnesota, and gravel pits around Duluth and Cloquet have produced some of the best (and largest) specimens. The area near Grand Marais, Minnesota, also produces many specimens with very fine sagenite formations.

Polished stalactitic agate

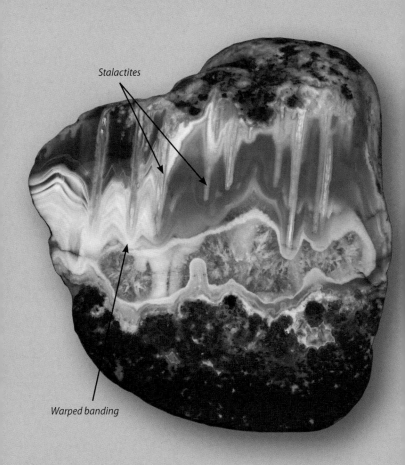

Stalactites

Warped banding

Stalactitic Agate

SYNONYMS: None

Primary Range

CHARACTERISTIC FEATURES:

- Slender, tapering, icicle-like growths embedded in an agate that extend from one side of the specimen and end before they reach the other side

- Chalcedony banding often warps and bends around the growths to accommodate them

- Very rarely, the whole agate itself may be a stalactite

RARITY: Stalactitic agates are quite uncommon; well-formed examples are rare

DESCRIPTION: When most people think of stalactites, they picture icicle-like mineral formations hanging from the ceiling of a cave, but stalactitic agates, which contain stalactites, aren't much different. Stalactites formed in much the same manner as tube agates (page 65). The cavities these agates formed in were also home to needle-like crystals of other minerals, such as goethite. As the agate developed, chalcedony collected on these crystals, eventually creating stalactites that extend partway through an agate. The common agate banding then bent and warped around the stalactites. But these embedded growths aren't the only type

Unpolished stalactitic agate

Stalactites

of agate stalactite in the Lake Superior region. Very rare examples from near Thunder Bay, Ontario, don't just contain stalactites—they are entire stalactites. These carrot-shaped agates grew within the cavities in limestone, a sedimentary rock less common in the Lake Superior region, and contain layers of chalcedony, quartz and calcite. Their outer surfaces are rough and crude, coated in soft, chalky calcite, but they are unmistakable. Whether your agate contains stalactites or is itself a stalactite, these agates are a unique and uncommon collecting opportunity.

IDENTIFICATION: It is very likely that you'll confuse a stalactitic agate with a tube agate (page 65) and vice versa. That's not a coincidence —they're virtually the same thing. In either type of agate, look for elongated tube-like structures that extend deeply into an agate. Very often, where the narrow structures meet the outer surfaces of an agate, there is a round structure resembling an agate eye (page 83), though, unlike agate eyes, these structures are not perfectly circular. In short, determining if your specimen has stalactite or tube structures is easy; telling them apart is not. If you're very lucky, your specimen will be broken or cut in such a way that the terminations of each stalactite are easily visible. Of course, the elongated structures should end within the agate, because if they extend through to the other side, the specimen is considered to be a tube agate. If the structures are more hidden or vague, however, your specimen is probably a tube agate, as they are much more common. On the

Agate stalactite

other hand, identifying agate stalactites from Ontario is easy, as they flawlessly illustrate the ideal shape of stalactites.

COLLECTIBILITY: Lake Superior agates containing stalactites don't garner much attention from most collectors unless the stalactites are well formed and obvious. The trouble with most stalactitic agates is that most cannot be definitively distinguished from tube agates, so while stalactitic agates are undoubtedly rarer, most buyers won't invest in one unless it is clearly not a tube agate. Agate stalactites from Thunder Bay, Ontario, on the other hand, are extremely desirable and valuable, thanks to their rarity. The quarry where they were once found, however, is privately owned and closed to collecting. This fact only drives up the prices of specimens that are already in private collections.

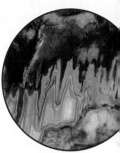

Polished stalactite agate

COMPARE & CONTRAST:

Tube Agate	Eye Agate	Sagenitic Agate
Tube-like structures extend all the way through an agate	Circular structures do not extend deep into agate	Inclusions are in radial arrangements

WHERE TO BEGIN LOOKING: Gravel pits near Duluth, Minnesota, have yielded nice agates containing stalactites. Agates that don't just contain stalactites, but actually are stalactites, are found in limestone near Thunder Bay, Ontario.

Polished black and white, impurity-rich vein agate

Vein Agate

SYNONYMS: Seam agate, fissure infill agate

Primary Range

CHARACTERISTIC FEATURES:

- Elongated banding patterns exhibited in flatter, broader agates

- Specimens often exhibit irregular rough edges rather than the round, smooth exteriors common on other agate types

- Vein agates are often still embedded within the rock in which they formed, making their long, narrow structure very apparent

RARITY: Vein agates are quite uncommon, but they turn up more frequently in northeastern Minnesota

DESCRIPTION: The vast majority of Lake Superior agates formed within vesicles, or gas bubbles trapped in basalt or rhyolite, but not all of them. Some can be found in a number of other settings, including cracks or fissures. Called vein or seam agates, agates that formed in cracks exhibit long, narrow banded patterns and irregular, often rough, exterior surfaces derived from the cavity where they formed. If only partially weathered, vein agates may also have a flat, broad shape reminiscent of the crack they formed within. Rarer examples may actually be found still embedded in their host rock, which is often rhyolite, as rhyolite's high silica content helps agates adhere more to the rock. But because vein agates can form within cracks in any type of rock, they can sometimes form in rocks containing no cavities and those that typically do not produce agates. For example,

Unpolished vein agate

Rhyolite

Crack-filling agate

a particularly recognizable type of vein agate from northeastern Minnesota is black and white and thought to have formed in rocks rich with iron ores.

Thunder Bay agates (page 137) are another variety of vein agate; they form within limestone, a sedimentary rock that typically doesn't produce agates. When acidic groundwater dissolved parts of the limestone, cracks and cavities developed where vein agates could later form.

IDENTIFICATION: Vein agates are one of the more difficult varieties of Lake Superior agates to identify conclusively. In many ways, vein agates resemble "normal" agates, especially when freed from their host rock or weathered enough that their elongated shape is no longer apparent. Those specimens may be impossible to identify as vein agates if there are no other available clues. To make matters more confusing, normal agates that formed in very narrow vesicles may resemble vein agates. Most of the time, your best hope for adding a vein agate to your collection is to find one still embedded in its host rock. That way, the vein-like appearance of the agate is well preserved and obvious. But those samples are very rare in the Lake Superior region, so you may want to turn your attention to Minnesota's black-and-white vein agates instead. While still uncommon, these agates exhibit thin white-banded patterns within a mass of gray or black chalcedony and are clearly a type of vein agate.

Polished black and white, impurity-rich vein agate

COLLECTIBILITY: Lake Superior vein agates aren't that desirable. Perhaps if they were more common they might garner more attention, but given their rarity, their often unremarkable appearance, the general difficulty of identifying them, and their poorly defined banding, vein agates are typically ignored and not considered valuable. But there are exceptions, of course. Specimens that are found still embedded in their host rock can be highly desired by collectors interested in rare Lake Superior agates, especially if the agate is brightly colored. But for these to be valuable, the agate vein must be obvious and unmistakable.

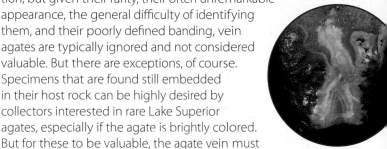

Vein agate in mass of hematite

COMPARE & CONTRAST:

Water-level Agate	Jasp-Agate	Fortification Agate	Thunder Bay Agate
Bands are horizontal and parallel	Bands are intergrown with jasper	Specimens are more rounded in shape	Specimens formed in limestone

WHERE TO BEGIN LOOKING: Gravel pits and occasionally riverbeds in northeastern Minnesota, particularly north of Duluth, yield black-and-white vein agates, while the shores of Lake Superior sometime produce vein agates embedded in rock. Limestone formations near Thunder Bay, Ontario, can also yield rare vein agates.

Exceptional natural water-washed agate

Extremely smooth surfaces

Water-washed Agate

SYNONYMS: Water-worn agate, river agate,
rounded agate

Primary Range

CHARACTERISTIC FEATURES:
- Exceptionally rounded and smoothed surfaces
- Specimen exhibits no hard corners, rough broken edges, or irregularities
- Chalcedony banding is typically visible from all sides of a specimen as the outer husk is generally worn away

RARITY: To a degree, most Lake Superior agates are worn and smoothed by weathering, but truly rounded and even-surfaced water-washed agates are fairly rare

DESCRIPTION: Shaped like the common pebbles of basalt found anywhere along Lake Superior's shore, water-washed agates are rounded and smoothed, thanks to thousands of years spent tumbling in rivers and lakes. These agates likely began their turbulent journey when the glaciers scraped them up and began shaping them. Later, as the ice melted, fast-moving water washed them away. Today, water-washed agates are undoubtedly the most collectible form of weathered agate and very fine examples typically command high prices. There are many reasons they are

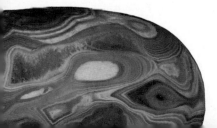

**Unpolished
water-washed agate**

No corners or pits

valuable. First, water-washed agates have had most or all of their thick outer husk worn away and exhibit copious banding on all sides. In addition, their smooth, rounded shapes are highly appealing. Because so many of their outer layers were ground away, water-washed agates also often lack the conspicuous flaws that other agates exhibit. But such weathering is not without its consequences; most water-washed agates are no larger than a fist, thanks to the large amounts of material removed from them. Many specimens are, of course, found on Lake Superior's shore.

IDENTIFICATION: Identifying a water-washed agate is not particularly difficult—after all, not all agates are so well rounded and smoothed. The real trouble lies in determining if an agate is actually rounded enough to be considered a water-washed agate. Many veteran collectors who specialize in water-washed agates won't accept any agate that isn't completely smooth and free of irregularities. So how can you tell? Since nearly all Lake Superior agates found free of their host rock have been at least partially worn and rounded by the glaciers, you'll have to take note of a few features other than shape. The banding on water-washed agates is a big clue, as it often wraps around to all sides of a specimen, whereas most agates only show one banded face. Also, the lack of a husk on water-washed agates means that there are no significant pits, rough surfaces, or other variations on their smooth exterior.

Unpolished water-washed agate

COLLECTIBILITY: The more involved you get in the hobby of Lake Superior agate collecting, the more emphasis you'll see being placed upon water-washed agates. That's because they are among the most collectible and valuable agate varieties from the region. In fact, some collectors build their entire collection primarily of water-washed agates and seek only the finest examples. Their biggest draw is the fact that they are surrounded by banding. Most agates have one face where the banded pattern can be seen, but water-washed agates are surrounded in swirling, twisting bands visible from all sides. The most valuable specimens are those with busy, wild patterns, contrasting colors, and completely smooth, rounded shapes with no breaks, pits or corners.

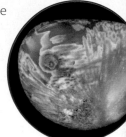

Sagenitic agate

COMPARE & CONTRAST:

Ventifacts	Peeled Agate
Brightly lustrous and pitted	Exhibit flat, evenly colored surfaces

WHERE TO BEGIN LOOKING: Lake Superior's shore between Two Harbors and Grand Marais, Minnesota, are very well known for water-washed agates (particularly just offshore), as are any shores in Wisconsin, Michigan and Ontario. The Nipigon Bay area of Ontario has been known to produce agates so water-worn that they appear polished.

Rare

Scarce and sought after, these varieties of Lake Superior agates are very difficult to find

Some of the most interesting and most desired types of Lake Superior agates are also some of the least common. Some of these varieties, such as copper replacement agates, are only found in one very small area, while others, like plume agates, are simply very scarce throughout the entire region, but all will take considerable diligence to find.

Copper Replacement Agate (pg. 121)

Plume Agate (pg. 125)

Rare Colorations (pg. 129)

Skip-an-Atom Agate (pg. 133)

Thunder Bay Agate (pg. 137)

Ventifacts (pg. 141)

Whorl Agate (pg. 145)

Exceptional polished copper replacement agate

Copper bands

Chalcedony bands

Chlorite

Copper Replacement Agate

SYNONYMS: Copper-banded agate, copper agate

Primary Range

CHARACTERISTIC FEATURES:

- Pale-colored chalcedony bands alternating between bands consisting of pure native copper

- Small size, typically no larger than an inch but very rarely up to several inches

- Found as whole nodules coated in soft, dark green chlorite

- Specimens often contain growths of other minerals, such as prehnite, epidote, chlorite, calcite or pumpellyite

RARITY: Copper replacement agates are one of Lake Superior's rarest agate varieties; these small agates can only be found in a few mine dumps on Michigan's Keweenaw Peninsula

DESCRIPTION: Of all the many varieties of Lake Superior agates, none are outdone by the amazing copper replacement agates from Michigan's Keweenaw Peninsula. These small agates, measuring no more than an inch or two, are extremely rare and are only found in a few isolated rock piles at the sites of century-old copper mines. In these piles, large boulders of solid basalt can be broken open to reveal tiny agate nodules still embedded in the rock. Why are they found in such an odd setting? The Keweenaw Peninsula was once the world's most important copper-mining district

Polished copper replacement agate

Agate eye

121

and mines dotted the landscape, digging deep shafts. As they removed rock, they put unwanted waste rock into countless mine dump piles. Three or four of these piles produce copper replacement agates in the form of whole nodules coated in soft green chlorite. Only when cut or broken do they reveal their incredible pale tan- or cream-colored patterns of chalcedony alternating with bands of pure native copper. They are thought to have formed when layered impurities of calcite dissolved, leaving voids between the chalcedony bands that later filled in with copper.

IDENTIFICATION: When cut and polished, copper replacement agates are truly unmistakable. But in the field they are difficult to spot, as they are found as small whole nodules with a thin coating of dark green chlorite, the mineral that originally lined the vesicle. Though they can occasionally be found lying loose on one of the few mine dumps known to produce them, most of the time the nodules need to be carefully broken free from solid, unweathered basalt. Even after all that work, there are no guarantees that you'll find one of these rare agates, and you won't know for certain until you've cut the nodules in half or ground away the chlorite exterior coating. There are so many other minerals and copper-free agates in the mine dumps that even a handful of nodules may not contain a single copper replacement agate. In fact, perhaps as few as one in twenty-five nodules will contain any copper at all, while only one in one hundred will have fine copper banding. If you lack the tools to cut and polish your finds, don't attempt to break the small nodules or you risk destroying them.

Polished copper replacement agate

COLLECTIBILITY: Copper replacement agates are found nowhere else, so it goes without saying that they are not only one of the most collectible varieties of agates in the Lake Superior region, but the entire world. And because the original source of these agates was deep underground, only a finite amount of surface specimens are available to collectors, which makes even small and poorly formed specimens considerably valuable. But it shouldn't be monetary gain that drives collectors to find specimens; it should be the incredible beauty, rarity and scientific importance held by these small agates.

Whole nodules

Specimen in basalt

COMPARE & CONTRAST:

Mineral Inclusions	Fortification Agate
Inclusions are not bands of solid metal	No bands composed of copper

WHERE TO BEGIN LOOKING: On Michigan's Keweenaw Peninsula, north of Houghton, the mine piles around Calumet and Kearsarge are known to produce these exquisite agates.

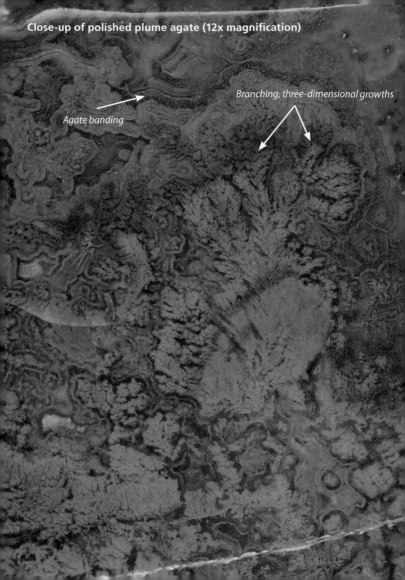

Close-up of polished plume agate (12x magnification)

Branching, three-dimensional growths

Agate banding

Plume Agate

SYNONYMS: Paintbrush agate

Primary Range

CHARACTERISTIC FEATURES:

- Small, very rare plant- or feather-like growths of red or yellow iron compounds embedded within chalcedony

- Unlike dendrites, plumes clearly exhibit a third dimension and under close observation can be seen to extend deeper into the agate

- Unlike dendrites, plumes form within masses of chalcedony, not on the surface of agate bands

RARITY: Plumes are very rare in Lake Superior agates, primarily because they are often very small and well hidden within moss agates

DESCRIPTION: Plumes are one of the most elusive types of mineral inclusions in Lake Superior agates. They are named for their seemingly organic shapes that grow wider along their length, much like a plume of smoke or a feather. At first glance, plumes may seem quite similar to dendrites (page 79), but they are actually remarkably different. Dendrites form in the microscopic spaces between agate bands long after the agate has formed and hardened, which makes them essentially two-dimensional formations. Plumes, on the other

Close-up of unpolished plume agate (14x magnification)

Plumes

Agate banding

125

hand, formed along with the rest of the agate. The plumes formed when particles of iron from the surrounding rock made their way into a body of still-soft silica (quartz). As the iron particles contacted each other, they adhered to one another, building a structure much like a dendrite. Unlike dendrites, the plumes were able to grow in all directions thanks to the soft silica that surrounded them. This is visible in many specimens because the plumes are often opaque while the surrounding chalcedony is translucent, allowing some depth of a plume to be observed. Plumes can be found alongside agate banding but more often they are well disguised within a moss agate (page 27).

IDENTIFICATION: Plumes may be the most difficult feature to spot and identify in a Lake Superior agate, and this likely accounts for their apparent rarity. The trouble isn't only that plumes are frequently very small—the largest rarely measure an inch long—it's that they form from the same iron compounds that also can create the moss in moss agates. This means that plumes are most often found hidden among moss agates' wild patterns, effectively camouflaging them and making them frustratingly difficult to spot. When searching an agate for plumes, magnification is crucial. Then, when you think you may have found one, look for the key characteristics of a plume: elongated, branching, feather-like shapes with perceivable depth. If your agate is too rough, cloudy, or opaque and you are unable to

determine if a possible plume extends deeper into the agate, it may be a dendrite. In this case, take note of the material surrounding the feature.

Close-up of unpolished plume agate (8.5x magnification)

Specimen courtesy of Eric Powers

Dendrites form between two agate bands, a trait which is normally quite obvious, but plumes are much more common within a larger unbanded mass of chalcedony with mottled, uneven coloration. Finally, it should be noted that finding plumes is considerably easier in polished specimens.

Plume (¹⁄₁₆") in white agate band

COLLECTIBILITY: There are many collectors of plume agates, and thanks to the popularity of much larger and better formed plumes in agates from other locations around the world, Lake Superior agate plumes are highly desirable by default. Though most Lake Superior plumes are quite small and difficult to see, collectors prize even poor examples simply for their rarity. Generally speaking, however, the monetary value of most Lake Superior plume agates is fairly low.

COMPARE & CONTRAST:

Dendritic Agate

Plant-like structures are flat

Mineral Inclusions

Inclusions are not plant-like in structure

Whorl Agate

Bands are wavy, irregular, and lace-like

WHERE TO BEGIN LOOKING: Plumes aren't found in agates from any particular area, but you'll likely have better luck in gravel pits near Duluth, Cloquet and Moose Lake in Minnesota.

Polished agate with rare color combination

Very unusual dark green coloration

Orange paint coloration

Rare Colorations

Primary Range

SYNONYMS: None

CHARACTERISTIC FEATURES:
- Chalcedony bands of unusual coloration
- Odd, rare colors in Lake Superior agates, including dark green, canary yellow, pink or purple
- Sometimes the color combinations are stranger and rarer than the individual colors themselves

RARITY: As their name implies, Lake Superior agates with rare colorations are quite uncommon, though they are generally more common in Minnesota than elsewhere

DESCRIPTION: Lake Superior agates seem to come in every color of the rainbow, but all of those colors come from the same source: impurities. In fact, nearly all the colors in an average agate—red, brown, orange and yellow—come from just two iron-bearing mineral impurities: goethite and hematite. Both occur as tiny, dust-like grains within the chalcedony banding of agates. But these familiar impurities can still sometimes surprise us. Unusually high concentrations of yellow goethite, for example, can result in an incredible canary yellow coloration and large amounts of hematite make for rich oranges and opaque blood-reds. But these are just a few examples of rare coloration in Lake Superior agates. With the addition of other, less common impurities in

Polished agate with rare intense yellow coloration

varying amounts and differently sized grains, even more compelling colors can result. For example, microscopic red hematite grains finely dispersed within white or gray chalcedony can create the illusion of pink or purple bands. Rare coloration can be found in any structural variety of agate, though many are fortification agates (page 23) simply due to their abundance. Whatever the rare colors in an agate may be, they can turn an otherwise mundane agate into something every collector wants.

IDENTIFICATION: To a novice just beginning the hobby of Lake Superior agate collecting, many colors may initially seem strange and unusual, but in time, after observing hundreds of specimens, it will become apparent that some are much rarer than others. In other cases, it is not the individual colors of an agate that are rare, but the color combination that is extraordinary. So what colors should you keep an eye out for? Greens are generally quite uncommon, whether they are dark and vivid or pale and faint, but be certain that the green coloration is within an agate's bands and not just on the outer surface of a specimen. A greenish hue on the exterior of a specimen is likely a chlorite or celadonite coating (page 13). Yellow colors in Lake Superior agates are not rare at all, but intense, vivid shades of canary yellow are. Purples are also extremely uncommon. But these are just some of the most exciting examples. Other colors, such as tan and pale pink are less conspicuous, but equally unusual. In the end, it takes experience to be able to identify rare colorations in agates.

Polished agate with unusual gray and orange color combination

COLLECTIBILITY: Agates with rare colors are all highly collectible and sought after by experienced and novice collectors alike. Of course the quality of an individual agate determines its value—everything from the completeness of banding to its macrocrystalline quartz content can affect value—but the addition of rare colors to an already valuable agate can make it significantly more valuable. The most desirable specimens are those that combine two or more unusual colors, such as green and pink, or those that juxtapose an ordinary, mundane color, such as gray, with a unique, rare color so that the resulting agate is unexpected.

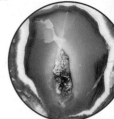

Pink and pale green

COMPARE & CONTRAST:

Paint Agate	Colored Macrocrystalline Quartz	Surface Colorations
Orange, tan or pink coloration in nearly all bands	Quartz crystals, not chalcedony bands, are uniquely colored	Odd coloration is only on outer surfaces

Rare orange and green combination

Specimen courtesy of Christopher Cordes

WHERE TO BEGIN LOOKING: Lake Superior's shore and the surrounding area near Grand Marais, Minnesota, yield strangely colored agates, as do the southern shores of Ontario and the sandy beaches of eastern Upper Michigan. The eastern end of Lake Superior produces pink and purple agates near Michipicoten Island.

Exceptional unpolished skip-an-atom agate

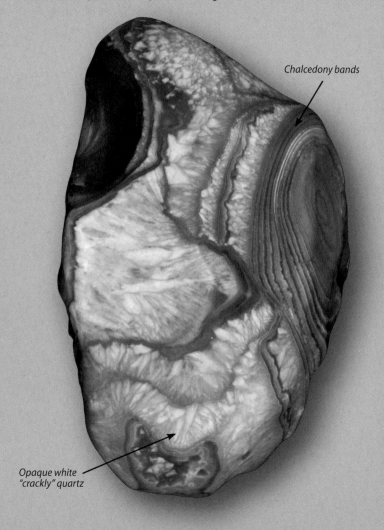

Chalcedony bands

Opaque white
"crackly" quartz

Skip-an-Atom Agate

Primary Range

SYNONYMS: Opalized quartz agate

CHARACTERISTIC FEATURES:

- Regions of opaque, gray-blue or white quartz with a "crackly" or fragmented appearance, often arranged into layers

- Chalcedony bands may or may not be present and can be any color

- There are typically no colorless or translucent areas

RARITY: Skip-an-atom agates are rare and typically only found on Lake Superior's shoreline, particularly in Minnesota, though few locations consistently yield specimens

DESCRIPTION: When most people hear of this rare type of agate exclusive to the Lake Superior region, they're often more interested in the name than the agates themselves. Both are equally bizarre, but the name should warrant less attention. These strange agates exhibit ample amounts of uniquely colored macrocrystalline quartz. Specimens often exhibit quartz in shades of grayish blue or white that are often layered, and typically have very little chalcedony banding in between. But what caused the quartz to look this way? Certainly it is not due to the quartz "skipping an atom" during formation, as the old collectors' notion states. Instead, it may have to do with an agate undergoing heating and cooling after

Polished skip-an-atom agate

Opaque gray "crackly" quartz center
Red chalcedony husk

formation. We know that the crystalline forms of chalcedony and quartz can change when naturally heated, so it is thought that volcanic conditions may have "cooked" already-formed agates, changing them into skip-an-atom agates. Primarily found in Minnesota on Lake Superior's shore, skip-an-atom agates can exhibit a variety of features, but those features are often inconsistent. Some have chalcedony banding while others do not, and some have bright colorations while others are pale. And there are non-banded skip-an-atom agates found still embedded in their host rock that seem to have almost nothing in common with agates at all.

IDENTIFICATION: Identification of skip-an-atom agates can be tricky due to their odd appearance, but there are a few key traits to look for. First and foremost, look for the characteristic opaque white to grayish-blue quartz and a fragmented and "crackly" appearance. Regular quartz can occasionally look similar but lacks the opaque qualities of skip-an-atom quartz. Secondly, unless highly weathered, many skip-an-atom agates exhibit the common husk (page 12) found on all banded agates. The husk can be of any color but is a good indicator that your strange specimen of quartz can be considered a skip-an-atom agate. But the real trouble with identifying skip-an-atom agates is that their features can be quite inconsistent. The best examples contain skip-an-atom quartz alternating between chalcedony bands or contain layered quartz, but these traits are only rarely seen. Finally, on Minnesota's Lake Superior shoreline, large masses of skip-an-atom quartz can be found still embedded

Polished skip-an-atom agate

Distinct layering

in their host rock, but most have no layering, no chalcedony bands, and no husk. Therefore, they technically are not agates, but since they exhibit the skip-an-atom type of quartz, they are often still considered as such.

COLLECTIBILITY: Some traditional collectors view skip-an-atom agates as a mere curiosity, but many other collectors have developed an interest for "weird" agates and skip-an-atom agates have become quite popular in recent years as a result. They typically do not command very high prices, but very fine examples with colorful chalcedony banding and pale blue opaque quartz can be quite valuable.

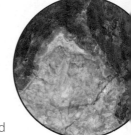

Skip-an-atom quartz in basalt

COMPARE & CONTRAST:

Banded Quartz Agate	Floater Agate	Fortification Agate
Quartz is not opaque	Quartz is not opaque	No opaque, blue-gray quartz

WHERE TO BEGIN LOOKING: Minnesota's Lake Superior shore between Two Harbors and Silver Bay is not only the best location, but one of the only locations for these agates. A few very rare examples have also turned up in gravel pits south of Superior, Wisconsin, and on the far eastern end of Michigan's Upper Peninsula.

Unpolished Thunder Bay agate

Attached limestone

Thunder Bay Agate

SYNONYMS: Thunder Bay vein agate

CHARACTERISTIC FEATURES:
- Irregularly shaped masses and stalactites of quartz and chalcedony within limestone
- Banding is often wavy and lace-like, twisting and curving wildly
- Generally colored white with shades of orange-brown
- Often contains soft patches or layers of calcite

RARITY: Thunder Bay agates are only found in one small area that is privately owned, making the agates very rare

DESCRIPTION: Just a few miles east of Thunder Bay, Ontario, lies a rock formation containing some of the most unusual vein agates (page 111) in the Lake Superior region. Most of Lake Superior's agates formed within vesicles (cavities) in basalt, but vein agates formed within cracks and fissures in rocks, including types of rock that don't contain vesicles. Thunder Bay agates formed within limestone, a calcite-rich sedimentary rock uncommon in the Lake Superior region. Because limestone is easily dissolved by even weakly acidic water, cracks and cavities often develop within the rock, providing the spaces where later influxes of silica-rich water could collect to form agates. But near Thunder Bay,

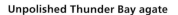

Unpolished Thunder Bay agate

many other minerals formed in these cavities as well, resulting in masses of quartz and chalcedony with countless mineral inclusions. The presence of these other minerals forced the agate banding to warp and bend around them. The vast majority of these inclusions are calcite, but in some rare samples, pendant-like mineral growths were completely coated by chalcedony, forming a stalactite, an icicle-like formation composed entirely of agate. Unfortunately, Thunder Bay agates come almost entirely from one particular location that is privately owned. Collecting was once allowed, and perhaps it will be again in the future.

IDENTIFICATION: Given that Thunder Bay agates are only known to occur embedded in limestone in one small area, identifying them is easy. You won't find any other agates in limestone in the Lake Superior region, and the vein-like nature of Thunder Bay agates is obvious. They typically consist of orange-brown shades of chalcedony with ample light-colored macrocrystalline quartz, often with patches or layers of soft, chalky calcite. The banding is very twisted and wavy, even lace-like in some areas. Stalactitic features (page 107) are frequently seen embedded in agate masses, as are growths like those seen in tube agates (page 65), though no inclusions in Thunder Bay agates are as straight and smooth as the ones seen in tube agates. Masses of Thunder Bay agate are typically blocky in shape and can be very large, and highly desirable free-hanging agate stalactites (see example on page 108) form within cavities in the agate.

Polished Thunder Bay agate with rare color

COLLECTIBILITY: Given their rarity and the greatly limited access to them, Thunder Bay agates are highly desirable, especially to those hobbyists looking to complete their collection of the least common Lake Superior agates. Some specimens can be very large—up to several hundred pounds—but as with any other variety of agate, bright, highly contrasting coloration is more sought after than size. Red specimens are the rarest color variant. But it is the extremely rare free-hanging Thunder Bay agate stalactites that garner the most attention. These icicle-shaped specimens rarely come up for sale, and typically fetch high prices when they do.

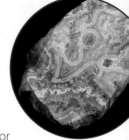

Characteristic coloration

COMPARE & CONTRAST:

Vein Agate	Stalactitic Agate	Tube Agate
Not found in limestone	Stalactites are embedded within agates	Elongated growths are normally very straight

WHERE TO BEGIN LOOKING: The mine where these agates were once produced is about 15 miles northeast of Thunder Bay on Hwy 527 but is now closed. The rivers and quarries in the surrounding area may also yield specimens, however.

Ventifact

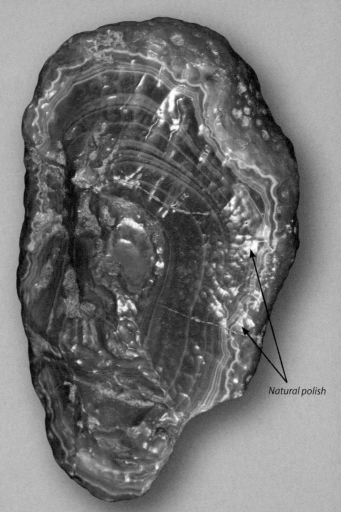

Natural polish

Ventifacts

SYNONYMS: Wind-polished agate

Primary Range

CHARACTERISTIC FEATURES:
- A brightly lustrous surface that looks almost polished; typically seen on one side of an agate
- Polished surface is very smooth and irregularities are often only shallow pits or small ridges
- Some deep and curving features may make a specimen look carved or sculpted

RARITY: Ventifacts are very rare and are not consistently found at any locality

DESCRIPTION: Lake Superior agates have undergone weathering for eons, and have been subjected to nearly every natural force. But some forms of agate weathering are much rarer than others, and ventifacts are the rarest weathered agates in the Lake Superior region. The word "ventifact" is derived from the Latin words for "wind" and "made," and while it may be a perfect description for how these agates get their unique appearance, ventifacts wouldn't even exist without sand. Sand, which consists primarily of hard, abrasive grains of quartz, easily becomes windborne, where it can travel at high speeds. Most of the time, especially in arid regions, the sand bombards soft exposed rock, wearing it away and sculpting it into unique shapes. But when the quartz-rich sand

Ventifact

Weathered surface pits

meets another form of quartz, such as an agate, material is removed much more slowly. As a result, an agate ventifact develops a natural high-luster polish, usually only on the side of the specimen facing the wind. This process is undoubtedly more famous for producing ventifacts from quartz-rich fossilized wood in the southwestern United States, but agates can also exhibit the peculiar pits, dimples and bowl-shaped indentations indicative of ventifacts. Agate ventifacts are extremely rare, but they are amazing example of agate weathering.

IDENTIFICATION: For all but the most seasoned long-time collectors, the odds are that you'll never find a Lake Superior agate ventifact. It certainly isn't impossible, but don't let your optimism cause you to misidentify a specimen as a ventifact, as they aren't the only agates that can appear to have a natural polish. Water-washed agates (page 115), which have been tumbled along rocks at the bottoms of rivers and lakes, can occasionally have nearly polished surfaces. Similarly, weathered agates with a fresh, clean break on their surfaces can also exhibit particularly shiny, waxy-feeling portions. But while water-washed agates are almost entirely rounded, and broken agates will likely have rough, angular edges, ventifacts are lumpy and irregular, but with smoothed corners. In addition, small, brightly polished bowl-like indentations are present on the surface of ventifacts.

Wind-carved "bowl" on surface of agate ventifact

COLLECTIBILITY: Lake Superior agate ventifacts are not without their critics. Some collectors are skeptical that it was wind-blown particles that polished these agates, and rightfully so; it would no doubt be very difficult to prove that it was wind that gave these specimens their shine. But by comparing the sculpted shapes and dimpled, lustrous surfaces of these agates with known ventifacts found elsewhere in the U.S., we can see that the similarities are undeniable. But whether or not it was the wind that buffed these agates, the fact remains that they are naturally polished Lake Superior agates, and that makes them highly collectible. As with any agate type, bright colors and beautiful patterns in a ventifact are the most valuable, while specimens that show little banding are typically treated only as a curiosity.

Natural specimen

COMPARE & CONTRAST:

Peeled Agate	Water-washed Agate
Exhibit smooth, but not brightly lustrous surfaces	Do not appear brightly lustrous

WHERE TO BEGIN LOOKING: There are no specific locations known for producing ventifacts, though the specimens shown here were found in gravel pits around Duluth, Minnesota.

Polished red and white whorl agate

Macrocrystalline quartz

Wavy banding

Whorl Agate

SYNONYMS: Hurricane agate, veil agate, feathery plume agate, disrupted band agate, cloud agate

CHARACTERISTIC FEATURES:
- Wavy, rounded chalcedony bands that often appear "lumpy" and seem to ignore the conventions of common agate banding
- Whorl-type banding is often arranged into semicircular or curving patterns
- Occasionally colored in bright shades of red and white
- Whorl-type banding often encloses a region of regular agate banding or a mass of coarse quartz crystals

RARITY: Whorl agates are fairly rare and are typically only found in Minnesota

DESCRIPTION: Whorl agates are one of the more puzzling varieties of agate from the Lake Superior region. On first glance, they may seem to look like common fortification agates, but on closer inspection you'll notice that the bands of whorl agates seem wavy, poorly defined, and arranged into almost semicircular curving patterns. In addition, the boundaries of each band may appear slightly jagged or lace-like, especially under magnification. In general, the banding in whorl agates seems to "break the rules" of normal agate band formation. What causes this unique banding? No one is sure, but it may

Large, unpolished whorl agate

Semicircular banding pattern

have something to do with additional chalcedony formations that formed within the vesicle prior to the agate. To make whorl agates more puzzling, some specimens exhibit whorl-type banding only on their exterior surfaces and have common agate banding at the center. Others have odd coloration and exhibit white chalcedony stained with "smudges" of intense red. Whatever causes these and the other strange traits of whorl agates is still a mystery.

IDENTIFICATION: Whorl agates have a fairly distinctive appearance that makes them seemingly easy to identify, and most are. But some specimens may not be so obvious and the curving, wavy bands may not be evident. Depending on how a specimen is weathered, it may not immediately appear to have the whorl type of chalcedony banding. If you suspect that you may have a whorl agate, observe the exposed bands very closely, preferably under magnification. Whorl bands do have a noticeably different structure from common adhesional bands and you can determine if your specimen is a whorl agate by looking for a lace-like quality at the boundaries of each band. In addition, most agates exhibit a distinct alternation between white chalcedony bands, colored chalcedony bands, and colorless granular bands. Whorl-type banding does not follow the same rules and generally consists of only white, almost opaque chalcedony layers. Finally, the coloration on whorl type bands can vary greatly, but typically appears as "smudges" or "smears" of uneven coloration that seem to sit on top of the bands rather than within them. Looking carefully for these details should help with identification.

Unpolished whorl agate

COLLECTIBILITY: While whorl agates are quite unique and very interesting, they generally aren't sought after by serious collectors. Their odd banding and often incomplete patterns just don't attract much attention. But as always, there are exceptions, and some collectors interested in "odd" agates seek out whorl agates. The most noteworthy examples are those that contain whorl banding that surrounds common agate banding. The contrast between the two banding types can make for truly unique specimens, especially when brightly colored.

Unpolished agate

COMPARE & CONTRAST:

Surface Colorations	Eye Agate	Fortification Agate
Uneven "smudges" of color are only on outer surfaces	Round structures are perfectly circular	Bands are smooth and evenly colored

WHERE TO BEGIN LOOKING: Whorl agates are typically only found in Minnesota. Look in gravel pits near Cloquet as well as riverbeds and lake shores all over northeastern Minnesota. Northern Wisconsin's shores have rarely produced specimens as well.

Oddities and Rarities

Between veteran collectors, novice hobbyists, and visiting tourists, thousands of Lake Superior agates are found each year and nearly every single specimen fits comfortably into the varieties described in this book. But that doesn't mean that the Big Lake's agates are without surprises. By taking the time to closely observe every specimen in your collection with a careful eye and some magnification, you'll likely find some strange structures that seem to defy description. While many of the odd features you may find cannot be explained by the current agate formation theories, there are others that are well under-stood. The following are just a few examples of the strange phenomena occasionally found in the region's agates.

SHADOW AGATES

A particularly popular oddity in agates is known as the "shadow effect." This occurs when very fine bands of dense, colored chalcedony alternate between transparent microgranular bands that are equally as thin. When light hits the dense chalcedony bands, they cast a shadow which can be seen within the clear microgranular layers. When many of these bands are very tightly packed, the resulting shadows can appear as dark ribbons that move as the specimen is rotated in bright light. This effect can be replicated by parting the pages of a book just slightly.

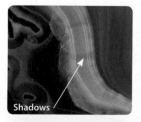

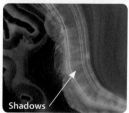

148

IRIS EFFECT

A beautiful and highly collectible phenomenon found in agates is the iris effect. Irises in agates are caused by translucent chalcedony bands that are so thin that light bounces between them in such a way that a rainbow-like spectrum of color is produced. However, this is generally only seen in slices one millimeter thick or less.

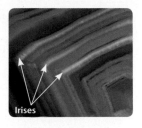
Irises

"SCRAMBLED" CHALCEDONY

There are many strange, unexplainable features in some Lake Superior agates, but one that turns up more often than most is "scrambled" chalcedony. Why the outer layers of chalcedony in these rare agates lack the usual structure and instead look "mixed up" and contain smears of color is a mystery.

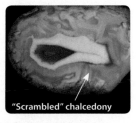
"Scrambled" chalcedony

Further Reading

To learn more about the science and mystery behind the formation of agates and the many unique varieties of Lake Superior's ancient gems, see *Agates of Lake Superior: Stunning Varieties and How They Are Formed*, also by authors Dan R. Lynch and Bob Lynch, from Adventure Publications. The book provides an in-depth discussion of the many agate formation theories from the past 300 years and how they relate to the many varieties of agates found all over the region.

Cleaning Agates

No matter where Lake Superior agates are found, millennia spent buried in glacial till or rolling around in rivers means that agates are dirty, both inside and out. Mud and dirt packed into the nooks and crannies on an agate's surface is easy to take care of, but iron staining deep within the cracks and in between macrocrystalline quartz crystals is a more complex problem. Most collectors are content with the agates as they are, but for those who wish to remove the dirty yellow tint from quartz and the dark brown stains from fractures, there is an easy and effective method that does not harm agates.

Always begin by washing your agates thoroughly with soap and hot water before letting them dry completely. This will take care of most exterior dirt. Then, carefully follow these steps:

- Spray your agates with a light coating of standard house-hold aerosol oven cleaner, making sure to carefully read the cautionary warnings on the can. Wear rubber gloves, and work outside or in a well-ventilated area.

- Place the oven cleaner-coated agates in a large plastic bucket. It doesn't matter if the agates are stacked or otherwise touching each other, and you are actually encouraged to prepare as many agates as possible.

- Cover the bucket tightly with a bucket lid or plastic wrap.

- Place the bucket in sunlight for about an hour to warm the agates. Similarly, you can place the bucket in a larger container of hot water so that the agates heat up.

- After an hour, scrub agates thoroughly with a plastic brush in soap and water.

Contrary to popular belief, you shouldn't use acids to clean agates! While occasionally effective, acids are dangerous, difficult to dispose of and can discolor agates. Oven cleaner can also be hazardous if used improperly, but it is a safer alternative, both for you and your agates.

Most agate collectors will eventually wish to polish some of their agates. While the subject of agate cutting and polishing techniques can fill an entire book and won't be covered here, novices should be made aware that the necessary equipment can be extremely expensive and certain polishing techniques can take several months, due to agate's incredible hardness. In addition, it is a popular misconception that agates are more valuable when polished. This is most certainly untrue when it comes to Lake Superior agates. While some poor agates can be improved by polishing, serious collectors typically prefer natural, unpolished specimens. As a general rule, only agates that show very little banding or are heavily damaged should be worked on; agates that exhibit beautiful patterns with well-developed banding and contrasting colors should left alone. Polishing them can drastically decrease their value and desirability. As an alternative to polishing, many collectors elect to give their agates an "always wet" look, since many of an agate's details and colors are more evident when wet. This can be easily accomplished by coating your cleaned agates with a small amount of mineral oil. Mineral oil, available in any pharmacy, is the only oil that should be used on agates; do not use vegetable-based oils as they will eventually begin to smell and turn your agates yellow. Wipe any excess oil from the agates and, when finished, be careful where you place your agates as the mineral oil will stain wood and fabric.

Glossary

AGATE: The concentrically banded variety of chalcedony

BAND: A distinct layer within a rock or mineral formation

BARITE: A soft mineral consisting of barium, sulfur and oxygen that forms thin, blade-like crystals

BASALT: A dark gray or black iron-rich rock formed by rapidly cooling lava spilled onto the earth's surface

BLEACHING: Exposure to chemicals that turn a specimen white

CALCITE: Calcium carbonate; a soft, calcium-rich mineral that forms six-sided prismatic crystals, among other shapes

CARNELIAN: Red or reddish-orange chalcedony, with or without banding

CELADONITE: A soft bluish-green mica mineral that forms as a lining within vesicles

CHALCEDONY: The microcrystalline variety of quartz composed of microscopic plate-like crystals arranged into parallel stacks

CHERT: A rock consisting primarily of tightly compacted microscopic grains of quartz and clay

CHLORITE: A soft, dark green to black mineral that forms as a lining within vesicles

COLLOID: A homogeneous substance containing large molecules of a substance suspended in another substance; particularly a gel

CONCENTRIC: Circular shapes that share the same center

CONCHOIDAL FRACTURE: Cracks with a circular shape

COPPER: Red-brown metallic element; element 29

CRYSTAL: A solid body with a repeating atomic structure formed when an element or compound solidifies

CRYSTALLIZATION: Forming a crystal; a mineral solution solidifying to form a distinctly structured unit

CRYSTALLIZATION FRONT: The forward-moving edge of a crystallizing mineral mass

DRUSE: A mineral crust consisting of many small crystal points, particularly quartz

ELEMENT: A substance that cannot be broken down further; elements are the primary constituents of matter

EROSION: To wear away due to weathering

FELDSPAR: An abundant group of silica-bearing minerals that are the primary components in most rocks

GEL: A jellylike substance; see *colloid*

GEODE: A hollow, rounded rock or mineral formation

GLACIAL LOBE: A rounded protrusion of ice extending from the main body of a glacier

GLACIAL TILL: The rock, gravel and sand deposited by melting glaciers

GLACIATED: Agates that have been worn and rounded by glacial activity

GLACIER: A slow-moving mass of ice formed in cold climates by the compaction of snow

GOETHITE: A black to brownish yellow hydrous iron oxide

GRANULAR QUARTZ: A quartz formation consisting entirely of small, compacted quartz grains

HEMATITE: A common metallic iron oxide that is red to black

HOST ROCK: see *matrix*

HUSK: The thick, outermost chalcedony layer of an agate that is composed of chalcedony spherulites

HYDROUS: Containing water

IGNEOUS ROCK: Rocks formed as a direct result of volcanic activity

IMPURITY: A foreign mineral within a host mineral that often changes the properties of the host, including its color

INFILTRATION CHANNEL: A channel by which a jet of silica solution entered a vesicle

IRON: A common, hard, magnetic black metal; element 26

JASPER: Colored, iron-rich varieties of chert

LAUMONTITE: A common, soft zeolite mineral typically found as blocky crystals in shades of orange, pink or gray

LIMESTONE: A soft, sedimentary rock comprised primarily of calcite

LIMONITE: The name given to mixtures of unidentified yellow-brown hydrous iron oxides

MACROCRYSTALLINE QUARTZ: Quartz crystals large enough to be seen with the naked eye

MATRIX: The rock in which a mineral forms

MESOLITE: A zeolite mineral that forms needle-like crystals

MICROCRYSTALLINE QUARTZ: Quartz crystals too small to see with the naked eye; requires a microscope to see

MICROGRANULAR QUARTZ: Microscopic irregular grains of quartz in a compact mass

MINERAL: A naturally occurring chemical compound or native element that solidifies with a definite internal crystal structure

MOLECULE: A group of atoms bonded together

NATIVE ELEMENT: An element found naturally uncombined with any other elements, e.g., copper

NODULE: A round, compact mineral formation

OXIDATION: The act of an element or mineral combining with oxygen to produce another substance; also *oxidize*

OXIDE: A combination of oxygen with another element, particularly a metal

PRISM: A crystal with a length greater than its width

QUARTZ: Hard, white mineral formed of silicon dioxide (silica); the single most common mineral on earth

RHOMBOHEDRON: A geometric shape resembling a leaning or titled cube

RHYOLITE: A light-colored quartz-rich rock formed when lava spilled onto the earth's surface

ROCK: A massive aggregate of many mineral grains and crystals

ROUGH: Collectors' term to denote natural, unpolished agate

SEDIMENTARY ROCK: Rocks formed of sediment, such as sand, at the bottom of bodies of water

SIDERITE: An iron- and carbon-rich mineral closely related to calcite

SILICA: Silicon dioxide molecules, often in the form of solid quartz or dissolved in a solution

SPHERULITE: A very small spherical formation

THOMSONITE: An uncommon zeolite that forms radial eye-like arrangements of needle-like crystals

TILL: See *glacial till*

VESICLE: A cavity created in an igneous rock by a gas bubble trapped when the rock solidified

WAXY: A mineral with the reflectivity of wax

WEATHERING: Being subjected to the forces of nature, such as wind, water and ice

ZEOLITE: A large group of soft silica, aluminum, alkali and water-bearing minerals that form in vesicles as a result of basalt weathering

Bibliography and Recommended Reading

BOOKS ABOUT AGATES AND THE LAKE SUPERIOR REGION

Carlson, Michael. *The Beauty of Banded Agates*. Edina: Fortification Press, 2002.

Lynch, Dan R. and Lynch, Bob. *Agates of Lake Superior*. Cambridge: Adventure Publications, 2011.

Marshall, John. *The "Other" Lake Superior Agates*. Beaverton: Llao Rock Publications, 2003.

Moxon, T. *Agate: Microstructure and Possible Origin*. Auckley, South Yorkshire, England: Terra Publications, 1996.

Ojakangas, Richard W., et al. *Minnesota's Geology*. Minneapolis: University of Minnesota Press, 1982.

Ojakangas, Richard W. *Roadside Geology of Minnesota*. Missoula: Mountain Press Publishing Company, 2009.

Pabian, Roger, et al. *Agates: Treasures of the Earth*. Buffalo: Firefly Books Limited, 2006.

Robinson, Susan. *Is This an Agate?* Hancock: Book Concern Printers, 2001.

Stensaas, Mark "Sparky," *Rock Picker's Guide to Lake Superior's North Shore*. Duluth: Kolath-Stensaas Publishing, 2000.

Zeitner, June Culp. *Midwest Gem, Fossil and Mineral Trails of the Great Lakes States*. Baldwin Park: Gem Guides Book Company, 1999.

Zenz, Johann. *Agates*. Haltern, Germany: Rainer Bode, 2005.

Index

About the Authors

DAN R. LYNCH has a degree in graphic design with emphasis on photography from the University of Minnesota Duluth. But before his love of the arts came a passion for rocks and minerals (especially agates), developed during his lifetime growing up in his parents' rock shop in Two Harbors, Minnesota. Combining the two aspects of his life seemed a natural choice and he enjoys researching, writing about, and taking photographs of rocks and minerals. Working with his father, Bob Lynch, a respected veteran of Lake Superior's agate-collecting community, Dan writes and produces their series of rock and mineral field guides and strives to create a relatable text that helps amateurs "decode" the complexities of geology. He also takes special care to ensure that his photographs complement the text and always represent each rock or mineral exactly as it appears in person. Encouraged by his wife, Julie, he works as a writer and photographer.

About the Authors (continued)

BOB LYNCH is a lapidary and jeweler living and working in Two Harbors, Minnesota. In 1973, he sought more variety in the gemstones used in his jewelry, so he began working with and polishing rocks and minerals. When he moved from Douglas, Arizona, to Two Harbors in 1982, his eyes were opened to the incredible beauty of Lake Superior's agates and he quickly became an avid collector. In 1992, Bob and his wife Nancy, whom he taught the art of jewelry making, acquired Agate City Rock Shop, a family business founded by Nancy's grandfather, Art Rafn, in 1962. Since the shop's revitalization, Bob has made a name for himself as a highly acclaimed agate polisher and as an expert resource for curious collectors seeking advice. Now, the two jewelers keep Agate City Rocks and Gifts open year-round and are the leading source for Lake Superior agates, with more on display and for sale than any other shop in the country.